The Two-Edged Sword

THE
TWO-EDGED
SWORD

Armed Force in the Modern World

The Reith Lectures 1981

Laurence Martin

WEIDENFELD AND NICOLSON
LONDON

First published in Great Britain by
George Weidenfeld and Nicolson Ltd
91 Clapham High Street London SW4

ISBN 0 297 78139 1

Printed by Butler & Tanner Ltd
Frome and London

To Jane and Bill

Contents

Acknowledgements

I am greatly indebted to a number of friends for help while I was preparing these lectures: to my senior colleagues at the University of Newcastle upon Tyne, for generously accepting my distraction from university affairs; to George Fischer, Head of Talks and Documentaries at the BBC, in whose hands the standards of Lord Reith are safe; to Tom Read, who performs the rare and remarkable feat of being all one expects of a BBC producer; to Shirley Fallaw for her indispensable support; and, especially, to Alison Pickard who, with unremitting patience and impeccable judgement, helped me at every stage of this complicated enterprise. Finally, I think I should break with the habit of a lifetime and publicly thank my wife for her tolerance during a period in which family life was sacrificed even more than usual to deadlines.

Preface

When I accepted the invitation to deliver these lectures, I had no idea that they would be broadcast in the middle of an acrimonious debate about nuclear weapons. This unexpected context has compelled me to deal rather more than I had intended with questions of the moment. I have tried to do so, however, against the background of strategic policy and debate that has emerged during the whole nuclear era.

I am exceedingly conscious of how much I have had to omit because of the extremely constrained format of six thirty-minute lectures. Sometimes the omission has been of a whole topic, such as terrorism. In other cases I have had to omit many of the historical illustrations that would have rendered my argument both more digestible and more convincing. Above all, I have had to omit some of the qualifications and reservations that I would have inserted in a full-fledged treatment. While I have agreed to publish these lectures as originally prepared – with the addition only of some passages left out at the last moment for reasons of timing – I am aware that their brevity can lead to misunderstanding. I think of my position as being in that rather dangerous place, the middle of the road. In the present somewhat emotional debate, however, I know that any refusal to endorse disarmament in general, and such causes as British unilateralism in particular, passes for militarism in many quarters.

Consequently, I should like to conclude this brief preface by reiterating my acknowledgement that the present strategic system is dangerous and that nuclear deterrence is peculiarly so, both because of the weapons involved and the inherent element of mutual threat. The trouble is that I do not find any of the radical alternatives plausible in terms of either strategic efficacy or political attainability. To endorse impracticable schemes and to bend Western policy toward them is likely, I believe, to undermine the system of security, imperfect but at least working, that we have already. It is also to neglect the lesser, more practicable ways in which we can make that system work better. Security, as I say in my last lecture, is not a matter of once and for all, but of more or less, demanding a never-ending effort to make the world if not safe, then at least safer.

LAURENCE MARTIN
December 1981

1 The Strategic Scene: Fact and Fancy

The Strategic Scene:
Fact and Fancy

Armed force is the ultimate tool of political conflict. It is not surprising, therefore, that contemporary military affairs are the subject of bitter public controversy. Perhaps the only uncontroversial observation I shall manage to make during this series of lectures – though it is by no means my aim to raise the temperature of debate – is to assert the supreme importance of averting all-out nuclear war. The problem is, how to do it.

Wars kill people and ruin countries. The nuclear-war strategy called 'Assured Destruction', for example, which is enshrined in the Strategic Arms Limitation agreements and, ironically, much favoured by some of the keener advocates of arms control, is actually *designed* to produce casualties of some 75–100 million on each side. Lesser nuclear wars are envisaged – of which more later – that might kill 'no more than' a few million; even, perhaps, 'only' a few hundred thousand.[1] Some point out that this would be no more than was suffered in many wars of the past – but these nuclear casualties would be incurred in a flash, with vast reserves of destructive power looming, unused, over the battle under circumstances scarcely calculated to encourage confidence in control and moderation. Nuclear war would thus, I believe, be a truly new phenomenon, and those who write articles on the subject under such titles as 'Victory is Possible'[2] – as some have recently – should, I think, find a different vocabulary to discuss such an unprecedented and ill-understood prospect.

I do not believe, however, that it is enough to make a simple renunciation of nuclear weapons, and that for two reasons. In the first place, important though it is to avoid nuclear war, that is not the only purpose of a national security policy. It is possible to

3

design strategies that offer a fair prospect of avoiding *both* nuclear war *and* many other unfavourable outcomes to international conflict – not falling, for instance, under the dominant influence of Soviet power.

In the second place, I do not believe that there is any *infallible* way to avoid nuclear war, even at *any* political price, now that the weapons have been invented. Experience should have taught us the difficulty of translating personal preferences for just and equitable outcomes into practical politics. I find it surprising that those who daily observe our incapacity to do much effectively about the chronic unproductive quarrelsomeness of British industry, can with such apparent complete confidence advance panaceas for the age-long phenomenon of international conflict and the immensely complicated problems of nuclear strategy. I must confess at the outset that I, at least, have no such complete assurance about the prescriptions that are, on balance, the best I can discover.

Beyond doubt, armed force is a dangerous tool, a two-edged sword, as likely to cut a careless master as his intended victim. The Western democracies are naturally averse to war. Preparation for war, and still more war itself, are ill-suited to societies preoccupied with material welfare and by no means all hankering for a military life. For at least three centuries, one school of Western thought has hoped that modern ways for man to enrich himself by trade and industry would make war obsolete.[3] The potential destructiveness of nuclear weapons led President Eisenhower to his famous remark that there is no alternative to peace, but this sentiment is far from wholly novel.[4] Even before the First World War there were voices prophesying devastation on an unprecedented, society-destroying scale and certainly few belligerents in either world war emerged with anything much resembling the aspirations with which they entered. Society reconciled itself to its sacrifices chiefly by supposing that it was for the last time, and it was perhaps natural that a writer fascinated by conflict and with the potential of technology, H. G. Wells, conceived the idea that the Great War was the 'war to end war'.[5]

We now know all too well that it was not. A glance round the world shows that war and armed force are far from out of fashion. It is endemic in the Third World, which is full of satisfied users: the rulers of recently reunited Vietnam, of Tanzania, India, Israel, Egypt and Mr Mugabe, all can point to a positive balance sheet.

The great powers are active there too. Recent studies by the Brookings Institution in Washington show that, besides the two large wars in Korea and Vietnam, the United States has exercised its military power in over two hundred incidents since 1945, while the Soviet Union has done the same on a little under two hundred occasions.[6]

The lesser great powers, like Britain, France and Japan, now dwarfed by the superpowers around which they chiefly huddle, constitute a zone conspicuous by the absence of much recent warfare. This is not evidence of the irrelevance of armed force, however, but of the relative domestic political stability that makes external aggression the only plausible means of effecting a change of regime and alignment, and of the deterrent aura of the superpowers that precludes such action. Armed force is not the less effective, however, for being latent in such situations. The postwar era of reconstruction and of economic boom may have exaggerated the potential of economic power as a rival to armed force; the former Japanese Prime Minister, Mr Sato, once boasted that his country was a 'civilianized' great power.[7] The panic with which Japanese statesmen greet American expressions of weariness with their protective role, however, reveals how far this illusion has been fostered only within a military balance sustained by others.

The prescription that is thought by many to have created this equilibrium and peace within the developed world, and to provide a brooding, monitoring shadow over the whole strategic globe, is 'nuclear deterrence'. There was a time, not so long ago, when this concept was pretty generally regarded as the crowning achievement of postwar strategic thought. The writings of such exponents as Henry Kissinger and Herman Kahn became set-books for college examinations.[8] More recently reflection has suggested that it is better to let such works run the test of time, like Bolingbroke, Burke or Hume, and that the celebration may have been a trifle premature. For it is becoming apparent that, in its classic form at least, the theory of nuclear deterrence has severe limitations.

The essence of nuclear deterrence – to which I will return in more detail – is that because there is no effective defence against nuclear attack, security can only be based on an unquestionable capacity and intention to retaliate in kind. In Churchill's now hackneyed phrase, safety was to be the sturdy child of terror.[9]

Now there is nothing new about the idea of deterrence; the

obvious ability to defeat an attack is a natural way to discourage its initiation. It is not even necessary to threaten defeat. Dr Jonathan Steinberg has illustrated how, at the turn of the century, Admiral Tirpitz' inferior German navy, by threatening the Royal Navy with more damage than it could afford to accept even for victory, was, as the title of Dr Steinberg's book has it, 'yesterday's deterrent'.[10] In much the same way the armed neutralities of Sweden and Switzerland are long-established examples of security sought by confronting a would-be aggressor, not with defeat, but with the prospect of higher costs than the prize is worth.

As we know, such strategies of deterrence have been tried before and have not always worked – it did not work for Tirpitz – so why do people pin so much faith on nuclear deterrence? The answer lies, I think, in the supposed potential *scale* of the costs and the certainty of incurring them. When Germany entered the two world wars, the possible high price of modern war was well known, but in each case German strategists believed they had hit on a plan to win cheaply and avoid the consequences: I mean, of course, the Schlieffen Plan and the tactics of Blitzkrieg. Today it is thought that nuclear weapons, in the absence of effective active or passive defences, prevent such delusions. It can be made clear beyond doubt that a nuclear power can wreak what we have come to call 'assured destruction' on an aggressor. Faith in this defensive posture has become so complete in some quarters that it has been thought our duty to persuade the Soviet Union of its interest in threatening unacceptable damage to the West and even to help her achieve the capacity to do so. Dr Jerome Kahan, for example, one of Dr Kissinger's agents in the negotiation of SALT and one of the purest propounders of its principles, warns us against 'anything that would threaten or appear to threaten the Soviet Union's retaliatory capability'.[11] Thus 'assured destruction' should be mutual – MAD, in the notorious acronym – and safety should be based on what has been cynically termed 'assured vulnerability'.

Unhappily – if that is the word – it is increasingly clear that this doctrine has serious and probably fatal flaws. At the very least, mutual vulnerability to massive destruction is an uncomfortable thing on which to base survival. One full-scale failure could be enough to destroy society as we know it, though my friends who are scientists tell me the global desert envisioned in Nevil Shute's novel *On the Beach* is not probable.[12] This is to live under a threat

6

from which men and states must inevitably keep trying to escape, if ever doctrine or technology holds out hope; yet efforts to escape strike at the roots of the theory of assured destruction.

Moreover, if the doctrine of mutual assured destruction is adopted in its full-fledged form, it promises a degree of strategic paralysis. Nuclear forces would become good only for neutralizing other nuclear forces. Yet great powers have important interests other than just not being annihilated, and have traditionally used armed force to pursue them. States seek ways to link military power to political purposes. So either nuclear weapons *will* be invoked, if only as an ominous, blackmailing shadow in political disputes or, if these weapons are utterly emasculated by deterrence, there could be a reversion to the uninhibited play of more traditional forms of armed force and conflict.

Thus the doctrine of deterrence by assured destruction can be relied upon to neutralize neither nuclear nor conventional arms, while its own mechanisms are subject to change as politics and science inexorably alter the context. Hence arise, I believe, the emerging controversies over theatre nuclear weapons, limited nuclear options, and all the currency of contemporary strategic debate.

The horrible potential of nuclear weapons and the faulty nature of what we might call the 'strategic' solutions to the problem have bred unprecedented enthusiasm for trying to abolish armed force or its components. It is not surprising that the innovations with which the strategists have tried to shore up the framework of security have become particular targets for keen disarmers. Unfortunately the approach to the problem from the perspective of disarmament and arms control – which I shall look at more closely in my penultimate lecture – is equally flawed.

The difficulty of abolishing, or even reducing or controlling, the weapons possessed by hostile or merely nervous opposing sets of states is well documented, and there is not time now to rehearse the obstacles to defining balances and verifying outcomes. Suffice it to say that despair about the complexity of designing and phasing partial agreements has sometimes prompted proposals to make a dash for so-called General and Complete Disarmament – GCD – within a few years. Such an idea is utopian, if only because the framework of most modern societies requires more organized coercive police forces for domestic purposes than neighbouring states

7

could contemplate with equanimity, because rearmament could never be wholly precluded, and because, especially in a nuclear age, illicitly concealed nuclear stockpiles, too small for discovery by inspection, could nevertheless prove decisive when revealed or used. Serious studies make it clear that GCD demands world government and even that would merely transform the problem into one of preventing civil war within the new world state.[13]

These difficulties and the lack of success in early postwar disarmament efforts, dramatized around 1960 by the development by both the United States and the Soviet Union of General and Complete Disarmament plans of patent insincerity, brought classical notions of disarmament to a low ebb. This predicament doubtless did much to inspire the conception, about that time, of the much more promising notions of arms control.[14] The original and essential essence of that much-abused term was an acceptance that armed force was not going to disappear and that progress would only be made by ceasing to deplore its existence and seeking instead to manage it so as to increase the chances that it would at least not produce unintended and uncontrollable effects. It was, and is, an essential element in the conception of arms control that the goal of harnessing armed force to rational and non-catastrophic purposes could be pursued by unilateral measures as well as by negotiated agreements, by carefully designing armed forces so as, for instance, to prevent unauthorized or accidental acts and to avoid unintended provocations of reciprocally uncontrolled or unconstructive behaviour by opponents. If common ground could be identified between states and made the basis for mutually reassuring agreements, tacit or explicit, so much the better. Such policies might not necessarily, it should be noted, result in fewer weapons or lower costs. The Polaris-type submarine-based missile system, for example, is generally regarded as a valuable contribution to several forms of strategic stability, but it was an innovation once, and far from cheap.

It is, I believe, a great tragedy that the concept of arms control, which was coined to designate these modest but intensely practical approaches to moderating the role of armed force in the world, has in recent years been perverted and invested with many of the illusions that bedevilled the idea of disarmament, so that many people are now quite insensitive to the distinction. Arms control, which should be an ingredient in any wise security policy, is all too frequently depicted as an alternative to such a policy. Far too many of those who feel an urgent need to mitigate the undoubted dangers of armed force and unbridled military confrontation, feel obliged to attack the very idea of national defence. Such attitudes breed intellectual confusion, half-truths and downright error.

To take a couple of related examples: it is continually asserted, or more often taken for granted, that we are in the throes of an 'arms race', a process in which ever-increasing sums of money are wasted on more and more, worse and worse weapons. Such races, it is alleged, lead to wars; an idea probably given currency in this country by no one more than Sir Edward Grey, the Liberal Foreign Secretary who led Britain into the First World War and who, somewhat self-defensively, wrote afterwards that 'the enormous growth of armaments, in Europe, the sense of insecurity and fear caused by this – it was these that made war inevitable.'[15] I would be more inclined to look for causes in the decay of the Eastern European empires, but, be that as it may, there is certainly plenty of evidence that arms races do *not* necessarily lead to war, and the role frequently assigned to the democracies' neglect of arms as a cause of the Second World War suggests the complexity of the issue.

Nevertheless, the phenomenon to which Grey referred, timorous mutual perceptions evoking counter-productive levels of armaments, is the commonly cited driving mechanism of an arms race. Some add an element of malice: the so-called 'military–industrial complex', the alleged conspiracy of soldiers and armament manufacturers, exaggerates the fears to promote its own political and economic interests. Sometimes, indeed, the proponents of that theory suggest that the arms are not related to *any* real external purposes and that the reasons for the continual build-ups are purely domestic. A recent careful, statistical study of the subject, published in the journal of the very anti-militaristic Center for Science and International Affairs at Harvard, concludes somewhat sheepishly but with admirable intellectual honesty that 'according to our data ... the presence of a nuclear arms race, far from constituting a given of international politics, proves to be a chimera. We have tried again and again to test for the presence of arms competition or arms racing and we failed to find anything each time.'[16]

Before everyone decides to give up behavioural science and try common sense, I should add that the authors do not mean, of course, that no one is buying arms; they mean they can discover no evidence that the rate of acquisition by one side determines that of the other. Such behaviour could still be a problem; at the very least it sounds a way to waste money. But the metaphor of a race seems hardly apt, and Blind Man's Buff might be more suitable. There is, however, a serious point, which is that the remedies for the process suggested by one metaphor would be very different from that implied by the other.

What behaviour would, in fact, be aptly compared to a race? It does not seem quite the best way to dramatize the fact that the percentage of American GNP devoted to the military fell from 9.1 per cent in 1960 (*before* Vietnam and *before* Kennedy's strengthening of nuclear forces) to 5.2 per cent in 1981, or that the military share of the federal budget fell from 49 to 23 per cent. President Reagan's much-discussed rearmament programme will, if implemented, put that 23 up to 24 per cent in 1982. Admittedly this proportionate fall is chiefly explained by the vast rise in social expenditure. In other words, the military establishment has not shared in the rising American standard of living. During the seventies American defence expenditure fell in real terms by just under 2 per cent a year. The sum spent on the most frequently discussed strategic nuclear arms was only two-thirds in the sixties what it had been in the fifties, and only two-thirds in the seventies what it had been in the sixties. In this country, British annual defence spending in real terms rose between 5 and 10 per cent in total between 1973 and 1981. As a proportion of GNP, defence spending fell from over 8 per cent in the early sixties to about 5 per cent today. It is true that in the Soviet Union defence spending seems to have risen by over 4 per cent a year in the past decade, but even that is much less than they could have managed; a recent estimate suggests the Soviet Union could raise the annual increase to over 7 per cent without going on to a war-mobilization footing. At present, Soviet expenditure is said – there is some controversy – to absorb about 13–14 per cent of GNP: President Reagan's programme would take the American proportion to about 7 per cent by 1986.[17]

But, let me be clear, I am not asserting that any particular level of defence expenditure is appropriate. I am merely suggesting that the numbers I have quoted are scarcely what the metaphor of an accelerating headlong race would suggest.

A somewhat similar and related point could be made by taking up – as I will again, when I turn to arms control in a later lecture – the rarely contested notion that there is a mad race for new military technology, that the new technology is usually worse, by rarely defined criteria, and that it is the West and particularly the United States that always leads these rounds of innovation. Thus, in a recent article in the *New York Review of Books*, Mr George Kennan – the distinguished former American ambassador to Moscow, historian and one-time Reith Lecturer – writes that 'it has been we Americans, who, at almost every step of the road, have taken the lead in the development of this sort of weaponry.'[18] This X is at best a half-truth and the half that is true is not patently disgraceful. It is true that the United States and the West, being more technologically advanced than the rest of the world, have pioneered in many areas and have used quality whenever possible as an offset to the large quantities with which the Soviet Union has equally sensibly compensated for its technological deficiencies. Not that the Soviet Union values backwardness, as its investment over the last few years of nearly twice as much as the United States in military research and development suggests. The Carnegie Endowment for International Peace estimates in a recent study that the Soviet Union leads the United States in seven and is equal in ten out of thirty-one broad types of military systems. This trend, by the way, has its encouraging side, as it suggests the Russians do not expect a war in the near future, for in confrontations where war seems possible it is obviously prudent, if the outbreak is expected soon, to mass-produce what you can, rather than to set out on long development programmes of what cannot be ready in time.[19]

But to return to my main point about military technology, we should not uncritically accept that innovation is bad. In a recent letter kindly inviting me and a great many others to an anti-nuclear conference in the Netherlands, the retired American Admiral Gene La Rocque, one of a small but not endangered species of anti-military retired officers, deplored the appearance of new nuclear weapons that are 'more precise and more devastating'.[20] Students of the subject will see an element of internal contradiction here; at least it all depends on what you do not want to devastate. With nuclear weapons, the way to compensate for inaccuracy is simply to use a larger warhead. Early nuclear missiles were very inaccurate; one, an early Cruise missile called the Snark, hit the wrong hemisphere on a test and disappeared up the Amazon. An increase in precision is thus a prerequisite for doing less devastation in aggregate, though the actual military target may be more certainly destroyed. Admiral La Rocque is not for complete disarmament and one assumes he would prefer military men to have some idea of what they are going to hit. Indeed you might even prefer the *enemy* weapons to be accurate enough to avoid damaging what he wants to spare, for we live in an age when, if war comes, it will be to the advantage of all to restrict unintended effects.[21]

At the very least, therefore, the answer to the question 'Is more precision bad?' is not *obviously* 'Yes'. The point about technological innovation – to which I shall return – can be briefly illustrated by another example. The submarine-based missile of the Polaris type is generally regarded as a contribution to strategic stability because of its immunity from detection; indeed some who oppose the proposed American MX missile as provocative, want an alternative put to sea. Yet the submarine missile was new once, and one suspects that, if invented today, it would meet much opposition because its undetectability would be said to run counter to the verification requirements of arms limitation. I recall the old lady who refused to fly, believing that people should travel by train as the Lord always intended. More respectably, I remember Clement Attlee's despairing remark before the war, that many of his party colleagues seemed to regard an ineffective army as morally preferable to an efficient one.[22]

Once again let me be clear, I am not claiming that new is necessarily better, or that there is not a lot of money wasted by people who think it is; I am merely saying that new or even more is not invariably worse.

That thought could be extended to suggest that any idea of the complete abolition of weapons is a pipedream and that if we agree with Aneurin Bevan on the foolhardiness of going 'naked into the conference chamber' we should feel even more exposed in that state on the battlefield. Given our modern and admirable demand that our means shall demonstrably serve our ends, the ideas at the root of arms control are essential and should be nurtured. But this demands their careful and realistic application to the problems of national security, not their transformation into unreflective anti-militarism or gratuitous denigration of ourselves and our allies. Such impulses, often based on generous and humane instincts, are dangerous, and the more so because of the unequal access popular movements enjoy in the Eastern and Western blocs. One can never know how naïvely oblivious to, or disingenuously aware of, this disparity propagandists in the West are. The European Nuclear Disarmament movement makes much of its appeal for support on both sides of the Iron Curtain, but my own belief is that the effect of such movements is inevitably discriminatory against the West, not merely because of the totally different situations so far as debate and influence are concerned, but also because it is the instinctive desire of Western liberals to hope that a natural harmony of interests will break out given the slightest relaxation in tension, whereas Communists make no bones about defining détente as a safer enhanced opportunity to pursue conflict with the non-Communist world. There is thus a Western temptation to give disarmament proposals a benefit of the doubt that is wholly lacking in many other quarters.

I certainly do not believe we should have a policy solely of 'confrontation'. Appeasement earned a bad name in the 1930s, and there are neutralists and unilateralists whose preferences would lead to its misapplication once more. But, properly considered, the concept of appeasement is a good one; by properly, I mean a due appreciation that others have security interests of their own which they are bound to defend, and that they may do so at no small cost to us. Trying to find ways to preserve our own interests without provoking counter-measures that increase our own difficulties should therefore be a constant endeavour. Thus I believe arms control should be both more and less than some uncritical exponents suggest: more, because it should permeate all defence policy; less, because it can never be a substitute for defence.

In my next three lectures, I will consider three important aspects of the current strategic debate – so-called 'strategic' nuclear weapons, the balance in Europe, and warfare in the Third World – before returning to the subject of arms control. I might as well say now, however, that I fear there is no 'non-strategic' route to security in a world of conflict. I often exasperate friends and colleagues by expressing issues in terms of cartoons I remember. Many of my listeners must have seen some of the drawings of the most famous cartoonist of the Great War, Bruce Bairnsfather. Bairnsfather's cartoons, you may recall, usually depicted a lugubrious veteran, Old Bill, and a raw and nervous recruit. In the most famous cartoon of all, Bill and the recruit are cowering in a water-logged shell-hole in No Man's Land under a barrage. The recruit complains about their plight and Old Bill replies, 'Well, if you knows of a better 'ole, go to it.' That, I fear, sums up my view of our strategic situation. It is a miserably dangerous one. But after some years of surveying the no man's land of strategic theory, I have yet to find a better hole than our present balance of power. Moreover, the metaphor holds when you contemplate the dangers of actually abandoning one system and moving to another. I fear the best we can do is tidy up the hole and shore up its sides. That task alone is enough to bear further discussion.

2 The Master Weapon

The Master Weapon

I remarked in my first lecture that the centrepiece of the contemporary strategic scene is something called nuclear deterrence. Many who find this doctrine alarming draw some comfort from the Strategic Arms Limitation Talks and the so-called SALT agreements that resulted. They must have received a bit of a shock, however, if they ever read the best-known account of the first SALT talks, written by Mr John Newhouse, a former official in the United States Arms Control Agency. Mr Newhouse, a great admirer of Dr Kissinger and his achievement of a SALT treaty, suggests that the underlying principle of the exercise was 'Killing people is good; killing weapons is bad.'[1]

This judgement, flippantly expressed, is deadly serious – in the literal meaning of that phrase. It moderates somewhat one's enthusiasm for a process of arms control that seeks to perpetuate such a system. Of course, Mr Newhouse does not really mean that killing people is good; he means that threatening to kill them is good, because he believes that such a threat will deter a nuclear attack on anyone with an obvious capacity to retaliate. Why does he think 'killing weapons' is bad? Because they might be the very weapons needed to kill the people, and their destruction might thereby undermine deterrence. The idea of mutual, mass killing, is, he hopes, unthinkable. Attacking weapons is not unthinkable, and by opening up the idea of nuclear attacks that are not immediately and utterly catastrophic, it falls into the category of what are often labelled 'war-fighting strategies'. Because these strategies suggest ways of actually using nuclear weapons, they alarm many people, who condemn the very idea as 'making the world safe for nuclear war'.

17

For all that, not many people can feel very happy about an alternative based on the idea that killing people is good. This is perhaps the classic notion of nuclear deterrence, which I briefly discussed in my first lecture. When, before the ashes of Japan were cold, the earliest thinkers about nuclear war hit on the idea that, if there was no effective defence against nuclear attack and if you did not wish to base your security on luck, or the forbearance of potential enemies, you had to rely on the threat of retaliation in kind, they all thought in terms of what came to be called 'city busting'. Why this was so, is uncertain. Perhaps it was instinctively felt, contrary to lots of evidence, that there is nothing governments cherish more than their people. Perhaps it was the consequence of most long-range bombing having been of the indiscriminate city-busting kind in the recently ended war, simply because of the inability to do any better at a time when less than a fifth of RAF bombs fell within five miles of the target. Even with atomic weapons, the scarcity of bombs, the limitations of aircraft and the erroneously predicted inaccuracy of ballistic missiles, made it reasonable to suspect that in a future war there would not be much choice about what to use as a target. There was certainly no serious psycho-political analysis of what it takes to deter.[2]

The classic view of deterrence has a supposed advantage, alluded to by Mr Newhouse. As there is only a finite number of cities, which are not very mobile (although their population can be evacuated) and the location of which is well known, destroying them may be supposed to require only a finite number of nuclear weapons. If all nuclear powers would agree to shoot only at cities, there would be no need to multiply and refine long-range nuclear weapons. Rational governments would thus have no incentive either to launch a nuclear attack or to start a so-called arms race. So convinced of the efficacy of this strategy were – and still are – its architects, that they both encouraged the Soviet Union to adopt it and condemned any measures that might impede the Soviet capacity to destroy Western cities. The capability for 'assured destruction' would be mutual, producing the doctrine now known to friends and foes alike by the ironic acronym, MAD.[3]

This doctrine, however, has several increasingly apparent flaws. In the first place, a doctrine of mutual deterrence, implemented in this way, requires nations to live for the rest of history with their survival entirely dependent on the good sense and restraint of their opposite numbers. Such a system seems unlikely to be one conducive to a relaxed international environment. A sudden change in government, an unexpectedly severe crisis, may overturn all expectations. Rich and inventive nations will surely be continually tempted to search for technical or doctrinal ways of reasserting greater control over their fate.

In fact, some such ways have already been discovered. The evolution of defences against ballistic missiles aroused a flurry of interest in the 1960s, and research continues; new ideas about lasers and other energy beams engender excitement about the medium-term future; spectacular improvements in missile accuracy and the multiplication of re-entry vehicles have reversed the arithmetic of offensive missiles, so that the odds now favour the several incoming warheads against the single missile in its launcher – and all of this begins to put a question mark against the fundamental assumption of inevitable vulnerability. We may doubt whether the defence will ever master the offence by purely technical means, now that the destructive power of the atom has been unleashed, if only because destruction seems to be inherently easier than creation. A toddler with a box of matches and a bit of luck could raze Versailles. But the combination of technique and doctrine is opening up a variety of at least conceivable defensive strategies. I pointed out in my first lecture that some deterrent postures in the pre-nuclear past had been undermined by the aggressor's conviction that he had hit upon a clever plan to avoid the consequences of his aggression. In recent years technological advances have offered at least the glimmer of plans to avoid the full force of nuclear retaliation. Yet to cut off such strategies by agreeing not to exploit the technologies in question was one of the primary purposes of the SALT negotiations.

Many people hoped that the willingness of the Soviet Union to enter the SALT process and to accept the treaty banning ballistic missile defence proved that the Russians endorsed the idea of strategic stability based on mutual assured destruction. It now seems more likely, however, that the Soviet Union gave up ballistic missile defence because their own system was proving disappointing and the United States appeared to be on the verge of a more promising breakthrough. There has never been much reason to believe the Soviet Union liked the idea of its own vulnerability. It goes against the whole grain of historic Soviet – that is to say,

Russian combined with Bolshevik - philosophy of foreign and defence policy to lay their homeland open to enemies and rely merely on their forbearance. Nor, indeed in the nuclear age, has the Soviet Union shown any inclination to regard population as a preferred target or nuclear war as a mere spasm of mutual annihilation. True, once Mr Khrushchev had broken the intellectual legacy of Stalin, the Russians very sensibly admitted that nuclear war might lead to the destruction of the leading socialist state and that war between the great powers should therefore no longer be regarded as a necessary step in the extension of socialism. Nuclear war should certainly be avoided. But Soviet spokesmen have always made it plain that should nuclear war come, the Soviet Union would wage it so as to minimize damage to themselves, so as to 'prevail', and ensure the survival of as much as possible of the Soviet centres of power. The point is well put in an article by Mr David Holloway, an expert on the Soviet Union and incidentally by far the ablest contributor, in my view, to Mr E. P. Thompson's well-known book, *Protest and Survive*. As Mr Holloway puts the Soviet view: 'If deterrence is not seen as foolproof, it makes sense to pay attention to how a nuclear war would be fought and how the survival of the state could best be assured in the event of such a war. In this context, victory retains significance as a concept: it is certainly to be striven for if war breaks out . . .'[4]

Some experts who have noted this perverse Soviet refusal to stop thinking about what would happen if a nuclear war actually broke out, have presented their discovery in ways that encourage the impression – particularly among those who do not read beyond the titles – that the Soviet Union might think it worthwhile to start a large-scale nuclear war deliberately in order to crush the West. Perhaps the best-known of these writings was the article by Professor Richard Pipes of Harvard, entitled 'Why the Soviet Union Thinks it Could Fight and Win a Nuclear War.'[5] The significance of this piece is enhanced for some by the fact that Professor Pipes became a member of President Reagan's national security staff. A closer study of such writings makes it clear, however, that the Soviet Union is extremely anxious to avoid a nuclear war and is certainly not working towards *Der Tag*, the day when it will be launched.

What is also clear, however, is that Soviet strategists, unlike many Western exponents of deterrence, refuse to regard the outbreak of nuclear war as an impenetrable veil beyond which thought and planning should not venture. Rather they regard nuclear war as a highly dangerous possibility, which might nevertheless occur. Should it happen, they think it worth preparing to do better rather than worse. Against that eventuality, the Soviet Union has therefore provided itself with a formidable array of well-adapted weapons and never suggests that these are in any sense 'unusable'.

It seems clear that the Russians would be loath to endorse Mr Newhouse's aphorism that killing people is good. Indeed, before it became convenient for the Soviet Union to sign the Treaty banning ballistic missile defences, Mr Kosygin, then the Soviet Premier, delivered some explicit and telling condemnations of the American proclivity for planning to kill people while the Soviet Union concentrated on defending them.[6] The current sharp debate about the future of Western nuclear strategy could not unfairly be described as a struggle over whether to persist in trying to educate the Russians in the virtues of assured destruction or to learn from them instead and adopt a more 'traditional' concept for nuclear strategy.

One reason for concern is, of course, the fear that, if the Soviet Union has a conception of how to fight a nuclear war to an outcome where they would 'prevail', while we only think of the outbreak of such a war as the end of the world, the Soviet Union may have a decided bargaining advantage in extreme crisis. The possibility that the Soviet Union has acquired the ability to eliminate the American land-based ballistic missile force so as to leave a weakened United States with no retaliatory options that would be better than surrender, is merely the immediate form of the more general anxiety.

There is, however, another reason for misgivings about an American strategy of assured destruction; a reason that goes back to another flaw in the original doctrine of deterrence I identified in the first lecture. The early architects of deterrence seem to have been so preoccupied with staving off a massive nuclear attack that they gave very little thought to why it might occur. Otherwise, they would have been quicker to recall that armed forces have been traditionally maintained, not merely to stave off threats to the very existence of the state, but also for protecting a variety of lesser interests and exerting political pressure on others.

The pure doctrine of mutual deterrence by mutual assured destruction implies a set of stalemates and the effective paralysis of nuclear forces. As there is no reason to anticipate the cessation of political conflict, the consequence is, as I have already indicated, either that states will continue to use the more familiar forms of military power under the umbrella of nuclear paralysis, or the paralysis will not be complete and states will invent, perhaps stumble on, ways to use nuclear weapons to pursue political conflict. Much postwar strategic debate has been in essence an exploration of these two possibilities.

They are naturally possibilities of the greatest possible interest to NATO, which has come to rely on the United States initiating the use of nuclear weapons if deterrence fails and conventional defences collapse. So long as the United States enjoyed a virtual nuclear monopoly it was possible to invoke the threat of all-out nuclear war – so-called Massive Retaliation – even for contingencies that did not threaten the security of the United States itself. This was the idea summed up in one of my favourite phrases from the mouth of the late Chief of the Air Staff, Sir John Slessor, 'The dog that we keep to take care of the cat, can also take care of the kittens.'[7] I do not, in fact, believe that many Western statesmen ever thought it was that simple, but undoubtedly the general sense of superiority made it easier to live with the theoretical need to strike first.

Once it was clear the cat the Soviet Union was rearing was going to be a tiger, the easy appeal went out of the metaphor. In a crisis, the United States might now face the dilemma characterized by President Kennedy as 'Holocaust or Humiliation'. An eager search for theories of limited war began: one such theory led to the build-up of conventional forces for the flexible response in Europe which NATO still espouses; another to a fashion for counter-insurgency and, by way of that, to the fiasco in Vietnam. I would like to look at some of the debris of those theories in my next two lectures.[8]

But already in the sixties there was the thought of using the large intercontinental weapons in limited ways. In famous addresses, a secret one to his NATO colleagues in Athens and a public one at the University of Michigan in 1962, Kennedy's Secretary of Defense, Robert McNamara, expounded a doctrine of 'controlled response': going after Soviet missiles while sparing Soviet cities as hostages against Soviet retaliation on the American population.[9] McNamara soon abandoned this idea, and turned to assured destruction, partly because it was proving impracticable to knock out the growing Soviet missile force with the technology then available but more because he feared the American armed services would have an excuse for an upward spiral of expenditure.

In the last few years, however, the idea of limited nuclear wars – what are called limited nuclear options – has come to the forefront of debate again. This debate is significant not merely for some immediately pressing problems of the Western alliance but also for the longer-term future of strategic theory.

The two things that have done most to reawaken the debate are the now unmistakable scale of Soviet nuclear armaments, dramatized and authenticated, as it were, in the SALT negotiations, and the recent dramatic refinement of nuclear delivery systems. At the outset, you recall, the case for making cities the prime targets rested in large part on the inability to hit anything else. In reality, the American and later the British armed forces always had a set of more specific industrial and military targets in mind and these target lists were elaborated in the McNamara phase of enchantment with controlled response. But the nature of the targets and the weapons meant that the difference was apparent rather than real: very large numbers of Soviet citizens would have been killed, and this was an accepted and very largely welcome feature of the plan.

Today, the accuracy of missiles opens the possibility of much more discriminating attacks. It is therefore possible to conceive theoretically of an attack on a few Soviet targets, sufficiently limited to leave the Soviet Union overwhelming incentive not to respond by initiating the city-busting war, but sufficiently valuable to make it desist, for instance, from a successful invasion of Western Europe. As with all deterrent strategies, the preferred purpose of such a plan would not be to execute it, but, by letting it become known, to deter the aggression that would provoke its implementation.

These are not just the idle speculations of ivory-tower strategists. They are the ideas toward which, with the general approval of their allies, several successive United States administrations have been moving. Beginning with Dr James Schlesinger, Secretary of Defense under Nixon and Ford, continuing under President Carter with the much-publicized Presidential Directive 59, and now under President Reagan, limited nuclear attacks with long-range nuclear weapons upon Soviet forces and even on Soviet territory have become a recognized possible component of American strategy.[10]

23

These developments greatly alarm many who regard them as in the vein of 'Making the world safe for nuclear war'. President Brezhnev, who is intended to be deterred by such talk, naturally scoffs. Just over a year ago, for instance, he declared that 'statements about alleged limited and partial use of nuclear weapons have nothing in common with reality'.[11] What are we to make of it all?

I start from the belief that we cannot escape the question by the total abolition of nuclear weapons. The problems of arms control are too extensive to discuss now and I return to them in my penultimate lecture. Suffice it to say now that, leaving aside the prospect of whatever more traditional forms of warfare might break out in a denuclearized world, the problems of verification and control entailed in schemes of far-reaching disarmament appear insurmountable. Assuming that abandonment of all capacity for self-defence will not appeal to the majority, I am left with the conclusion that some element of nuclear deterrence will remain a feature of the strategic scene.

If that is to be so, I hope it is not just a professional deformation of perception contracted from excessive exposure to strategic theory that leads me to feel uneasy about the idea of having no ideas about the use of nuclear weapons beyond threatening to kill as many people as possible because that is cheap and easy.

In all efforts to deter by the prospect of retaliation, I think one must grapple with a continuum of threats, the opposite poles of which I think of as Plausibility and Horror. That is to say, we have to choose between trying to deter by making lesser threats, which by reason of *being* lesser, are rather credible, or by uttering dire threats which, though implausible because of their awful consequences, are, for the very same reason, quite daunting – provided of course that we have some means of executing them.

So far, the nuclear powers have exercised great caution in confrontations with each other. Apparently even a rather vaguely diffused fear of nuclear war is a powerful force for moderation in crisis. But thinking, as we must, of a world that will probably come to contain an increasing number of nuclear powers, of a world in which serious and unpredictable crises will doubtless occur, a world which may even have experienced further uses of nuclear weapons to break the taboo observed since 1945, it would be irresponsible not to have plans for trying to limit the damage once nuclear weapons are used. So long as there is deterrence there is no denying it may fail.

In the specific contemporary case of the Western alliance, there are particular reasons for thinking more seriously about what would happen if deterrence did fail. To have no vision other than immediate mutual annihilation must surely sap confidence and cohesion in crisis. Given Europe's present dependence on American guarantees it must be divisive, as we can see in the current Cruise-missile dispute, if all the efforts to build 'flexibility' into response are in the area of theatre conflict, while intercontinental war remains a no-go area. Nor can we ignore the apparent Soviet interest in efforts to improve the outcome of nuclear wars. For, while enemies are fought on one's own best strategic judgement, they are deterred in terms of their *own* strategic assumptions, by military doctrines and postures that are impressive by *their* standards.

A frequent objection to preparations for fighting nuclear wars short of a simple orgy of mutual destruction, is that they encourage an arms race. It is true that the facile notion of 'overkill' has arisen in the context of planning simply to kill undefended people. Subtler strategies demand more careful analysis of the forces required. In reality, of course, even attacks on cities depend for certainty on a complex set of assumptions about the reliability and vulnerability of weapons and about a wide range of conceivable measures to minimize damage. Shifting the initial focus to more limited, probably military, targets need not greatly aggravate the problem. There is, for instance, no need to include enemy missiles in the target plan of a limited nuclear strike and several good reasons not to do so, particularly the need to avoid provoking a precipitate response on the well-known strategists' principle of 'if you're going to lose it, use it'.

The more plausible strategies of limited nuclear war envisage such targets as oil refineries, communications or conventional military installations. Targets of this kind are almost as 'finite' as the cities and, in any case, no more than a few could be attacked with much reasonable expectation of continued limitation. Multiplication of weapons is thus not a prerequisite for limited nuclear strategies and there are in any case, as I have already argued, many competing demands both military and civilian to limit the share of national resources devoted to nuclear weapons.

Once more, let me make myself quite clear. I believe the

modification of concepts of nuclear deterrence involves important issues that should be better understood and that the outcome of the debate will have a fundamental effect on the future military scene. Like all nuclear deterrence strategies, the idea of limited nuclear options is intended not to fight war but to deter aggression and thereby avert wars. Nevertheless I do not pretend to any excessive confidence in the idea.

For one thing, control would be far from easy. It would be unforgivable to pretend that a limited nuclear war would be very limited by commonsense standards, unless a single demonstrative weapon is envisaged. An attack on the Baku oilfields in the Caucasus, for instance, trying to minimize casualties, is estimated to entail 200,000 deaths and 750,000 injuries. A Soviet attack on the American land-based Minuteman missile force might hold casualties to 300–800,000 deaths. Although these numbers are much, much lower than the tens of millions of deaths deliberately sought by strategies of assured destruction, they are still horrific. Moreover the low estimates are optimistic, because there are so many uncertainties about the effects of nuclear weapons. These can vary wildly, according to weapon performance, weather, season and the degree of protection enjoyed, perhaps accidentally, by the population. The *worst* estimate for an attack on the American Minutemen is around 20 million. Some of the nuclear effects, like electro-magnetic pulse, may damage the very communications with which we hope the enemy will exercise his restraint.[12]

I conclude from all this that limited nuclear options are a dreadfully dangerous idea; a two-edged sword indeed. If such an option is ever implemented we shall be in a desperate plight. But for this very reason, I do not believe such strategies 'make the world safe for nuclear war'. Quite enough horror, quite enough suffused fear of holocaust, would survive to inculcate caution, while the consequences of the failure of deterrence *might* be infinitely preferable to those entailed by assured destruction. So I see the limited options as a few added stopping-places, none too hopeful but very much needed stopping-places, on the dreadful escalatory slope.

A crucial question remains: Would the Soviet Union play this game? They usually say 'No'. But their interest, their constantly reiterated assertion that war must be wielded as an instrument of policy, the high value they place on the survival of Soviet power – all this gives them a strong incentive to keep the course of war under control if it comes, while the technical apparatus of command and control with which they have provided themselves suggests a strong determination to retain the discretion of the high command.[13]

It is a further consideration, that strategies for extending control and selectivity into the period after nuclear war begins – so-called intrawar deterrence – are probably better suited than simpler, spasmodic mutual annihilation of the assured deterrence variety for adapting to the probable proliferation of nuclear weapons. A variety of possible opponents would seem to call for more than one undifferentiated response to attack.

Controlled strategies that avoid killing people as a matter of principle, even though they may be killed inadvertently, would also be less incompatible with, and indeed might be greatly facilitated by, the evolution of effective means of strategic defence. As the Russians used to insist, money spent on defensive weapons seems inherently preferable to that spent on offence, once you realize that one competes with the other within defence budgets that do have limits, however high.

I realize that the very idea of maintaining forces that could kill millions is repugnant on moral grounds. Morality is not readily quantified, but most of us seem to feel Hitler was all the worse because it was six million rather than six. Can any strategy be justified that requires even a conditional readiness to kill or risk killing very large numbers of people?

I do not rate myself very highly as a moralist and I will not argue with anyone who professes an aversion to any warfare, though I have some doubt about the success of such people in ordering their whole life in a manner fully consistent with that principle. Others, however, who will not go that far, feel there is something special about the potential destructiveness of nuclear war and cannot imagine any political purpose that could make recourse to it worthwhile. Such a war breaches the notion of proportionality that seems to pervade most of our thinking about justifiability in conflict.

To this I would reply, with some trepidation, that, if I take what I believe to be a Protestant Christian view, I do not *expect* to find a politically practical course of action that is without a degree of sinfulness. I can only try to select the least sinful of the courses open to me, never forgetting, however, that it is not rendered blemishless merely because it is the best I can do.

27

Because nuclear weapons exist and, as I have said earlier, cannot be eliminated – at the very least the knowledge of how to make them can never be erased – I do not believe that *any* policy can provide an absolute assurance that it will not lead to nuclear war. As the 1930s illustrated, even policies of military neglect and diplomatic self-abnegation can later be accused by history of complicity in causing wars. Consequently, I believe we do not have the luxury of choosing a policy wholly untainted by the nuclear danger. We can only choose between policies that entail different degrees of risk.

I can therefore see no absolute moral bar to the policies that strategic and political analysis lead me to think have the best chance of averting catastrophe. As far as I can see, a policy of sustained nuclear deterrence, combined with efforts to extend responsible political control over military action both before and after war breaks out – such a policy has as good a chance as many, and better than most, strategies for preventing nuclear war. In the meantime, it can make a useful contribution to preserving other Western interests. Moreover, I believe that the validity of this conception is not confined to the West and that combining the traditional logic of strategy with the new and revolutionary technology produces prudent rules of general application.

I recognize, of course, that today's strategic thinking is time- and culture-bound. Even if it is adequate I do not doubt that technological and political change will demand fresh strategic speculation and new security policies. I shall be very much surprised, however, if it ever comes to seem wise to observe such a sharp distinction between nuclear deterrence and the more traditional realms of strategy as the advocates of Mutual Assured Destruction attempted. Indeed, as I intend to argue in my next lecture, nuclear deterrence depends on much more than nuclear weapons – on the proper marriage of those weapons to an infrastructure of military and political power.

3 The European Balance

The European Balance

Dangerous though it is, the strategic nuclear balance at least has the merit that its dangers are obvious and promote a great deal of salutary caution. It therefore seems much more likely that, if nuclear war ever does break out between the major powers, it will be as the result of miscalculation in some local confrontation rather than a 'bolt from the blue', launched because the strategic balance suddenly looks favourable to one side or the other. Doctrines for the graduated use of strategic nuclear weapons, of the kind I discussed in the last lecture, may do something to enhance their deterrent effect over such confrontations, but they remain clumsy and dangerous instruments. To make nuclear deterrence effective consequently requires a framework of more traditional military capability, that can be more readily applied to specific strategic contingencies.

By far the most important potential arena for such conflicts is Europe, where the interests of the superpowers are most clearly defined and where the most powerful military forces in history have been concentrated. If nuclear deterrence is the doctrinal centrepiece of contemporary strategy, Europe is its geopolitical focus.

I must admit at the start I would have discussed the European strategic scene with rather more confidence a couple of years ago than I do today. Events in Poland and the rise of neutralist or unilateralist sentiment in Western Europe remind us how the political elements in a military balance can change much more rapidly than the material.

The North Atlantic Alliance is a response to the final collapse in 1945 of the self-contained European balance of power. After the First World War, it took a decade or more before the next clear danger to European security manifested itself; so much so that the RAF was reduced to measuring itself against a war with France. In 1945, with the Red Army west of Berlin, there was no room to doubt that, if a danger existed, it came from the Soviet Union. The North Atlantic Treaty called in American power to redress the balance. It explains a lot of subsequent history to note that the Treaty was signed in April 1949: that is, before the Soviet Union had exploded an atomic bomb; before the United States had decided that the thermonuclear weapon – the H-bomb – was feasible.

There is remarkable unanimity among Western sovietologists about what Soviet aims in Europe have been consistently since 1945. First priority is maintenance of hegemony over Eastern Europe both for strategic reasons and because of its ideological significance as an established part of the socialist camp. Second comes the reduction of American power and presence in Western Europe and their replacement by those of the Soviet Union itself though not necessarily by assuming the burden of actual occupation. The expulsion of the United States is not to be pursued, however, in such a manner as to create a self-reliant Western Europe, especially not one under West German leadership.[1]

This theme of breaking down the barrier created by the Western alliance runs through all postwar Soviet diplomacy, whether in the area of arms control or of East–West trade. Presented in the guise of 'normalizing' relations, the theme finds echoes in the West. To an extent this is understandable. A power the size of the Soviet Union, which unlike the United States is a geographical part of Europe, cannot be denied a role in European affairs. The Harmel Report, commissioned by NATO in 1967, suggested that the appropriate formula was détente *and* defence. This is wise but difficult; rather, as Mr Dean Acheson once said to me, like asking a man to breathe in and out at the same time. In theory, keeping up one's guard while exploring the room for compromise are compatible, even complementary, exercises. Unfortunately the two are hard to reconcile in democracies, as we have seen in the disarray caused by efforts to implement sanctions after the repressive Soviet action in Czechoslovakia and Afghanistan.

By nature, an alliance is a rational precaution against a threat: it can be destroyed either by concluding that the threat is too small to worry about or by deciding it is too big to handle. In a nuclear Europe both sentiments often combine to erode the defensive will.

Against such a background the Polish crisis is dangerous for NATO as well as the Warsaw Pact. To lose Poland would be a bitter ideological and strategic blow for the Soviet Union. Hitherto the Soviet Union has tried to ensure that no gain of socialism is reversed; President Brezhnev raised this to an explicit principle in the doctrine that bears his name. True, Yugoslavia got away, at least for the moment. Hungary, Czechoslovakia and Afghanistan did not. Poland's fate remains undecided.

It is not my place to explore the political possibilities further, but to look at the strategic implications. If the Soviet army crushes the Poles, NATO will be back in a familiar situation. The Soviet Union may be less sure of its lines of communication and, for a time at least, unable to rely on the Polish army. NATO may become somewhat more lively in its military preparations. But previous episodes – Hungary, Czechoslovakia, Afghanistan – do not suggest the stimulus would be lasting.

But if the Poles do prevail, and establish their relative independence, it will at least superficially be a considerable victory for the West; the first 'roll-back' of Soviet power in Europe since the Austrian peace treaty and by far the most important. But there will be danger for the West as well. Neutralists and unilateralists would be quick to point to it as evidence of the reasonableness of the Soviet Union and the powerlessness of the Soviet army. If this opinion eroded European contributions to NATO, a reciprocal wave of 'Mansfieldism' in the United States – the belief that American troops in Europe should be substantially reduced – might well loosen the American commitment. That prospect I would find highly alarming, for it is far from certain that any Soviet retreat would be permanent or that it would necessarily be so very fatal to Soviet military capability. Already Polish trade unionists have understandably said, for instance, that Poland must continue to guarantee the Soviet Union's rights of military access and transit.

So I conclude that the maintenance of the framework of Western European defence would be just as necessary after a happy outcome for the Poles as after a less happy one. Indeed, I believe that Western military strength and the existence of a Western alliance sufficiently coherent at least to threaten plausible economic and political reprisals are an important precondition for Polish success, and for any further evolution of freedom in Eastern Europe.

In view of his recent criticism of allegedly excessive Western fondness for military preparation and innovation, which I quoted in my first lecture, I found it interesting to turn to Mr George Kennan's own Reith Lectures, delivered more than twenty years ago as an influential appeal for *rapprochement* in Central Europe. *Some* people suggested, said Mr Kennan, that because the Soviet Union seemed unlikely to launch a gratuitous attack on Western Europe, the 'Western military structure could be dismantled'. 'What utter nonsense!' declared Mr Kennan. 'As though we did not know that any sudden and unilateral disarmament would create new political situations and new invitations to aggression where none existed before. Armaments are important, not just for what could be 'done with them in time of war, but for the psychological shadows they cast in time of peace.'[2]

Since 1945, the chief shadow in Europe has been cast by the Soviet army. The orthodox Western view has been that NATO cannot cope with the Soviet army in a full-scale conventional war. For most of the postwar years the Soviet army has fielded much larger quantities of divisions and weapons than NATO, but NATO has been able to console itself with higher quality. There is not time for me to bore you with all the much-publicized evidence for believing that while the Soviet *quantitative* advantage has, if anything, grown even greater during the seventies, the West's *qualitative* edge has been seriously eroded and in some instances reversed. To take tank forces (the most frequently cited index of strength and crucial to the success of a modern invading force), the Warsaw Pact's advantage over NATO on the Central Front has risen from 16,000 tanks to NATO's 6,000 in 1972, to a margin of 20,000 to NATO's 7,000 today. At the same time the Soviet Union has reversed the traditional pattern in which each new technical sophistication has usually appeared first on the Western side. Thus the Soviet Union introduced the so-called 'fourth generation' tank – that is, the one after the Chieftain–Leopard generation – *before* NATO. Indeed the Soviet Union produced 2,500 of these new tanks in 1980 alone, and already has more of this generation deployed than NATO *plans* to have by the mid-1980s.

Similar points could be made about other elements in the conventional balance, including air forces. But rather than reel off more statistics, every one of which can be argued over at length, let me content myself with quoting the conclusion of the latest *Military*

Balance published by the International Institute for Strategic Studies, a Western organization it is true, but one certainly not given to alarmism. After a careful survey of the evidence, the Institute concludes:

> The numerical balance over the last twenty years has slowly but steadily moved in favour of the East. At the same time the West has largely lost the technological edge which allowed NATO to believe that quality could substitute for numbers. One cannot conclude from this that NATO would suffer defeat in war, but one can conclude that there has been sufficient danger in the trend to require urgent remedies.[3]

This impression is clearly filtering down to a wider public. In a recent opinion poll, more than half of the respondents believed that the Soviet Union was the 'world's strongest military power', compared to a quarter who believed that about the United States; similarly over half thought the Soviet Union had more nuclear weapons than any other country, while under a quarter thought that to be true of America.

The Institute for Strategic Studies qualifies the pessimistic conclusion about the trend over the past twenty years by observing that even with its increased margin of superiority, the Soviet Union cannot yet be certain of a quick and easy victory and must therefore still feel deterred from aggression. How much comfort you derive from that, depends on how you envisage the outbreak of war in Europe. Soviet military doctrine does lay great stress on military 'norms': that is, on theoretically established levels of force necessary for success in particular types of operation.[4] This is, however, an ideal, and does not mean they might not take a chance if political imperatives so dictated. Wars are often started not out of confident ambition but out of despair about the prospects envisaged otherwise. The Japanese attacked Pearl Harbor not only with inferior forces but even without great confidence in winning. The same was true of the Egyptians in the 1973 war against Israel. I have even heard it said by a great expert on Soviet affairs, that, if the Soviet Union decided to invade Poland, it might be tempted to carry on and launch at least a limited attack on NATO so as to turn a dangerous internal dispute, disruptive of Soviet Army morale, into a crusade against external foes.

Moreover, military balances are tricky things, partly in the eye of the beholder. Hitler attacked France in 1940 and Russia in 1941 with forces materially inferior but strategically and tactically better managed. The crude material balance of men and machines takes effect only through the mechanisms of military and political skill and determination. Here again is the phenomenon I referred to in an earlier lecture: the instability of conventional military balances, and the particular danger arising from the would-be aggressor who believes he has hit on a 'plan'.

The device NATO relies upon to replace this dangerous imprecision with deterrent certainty is the nuclear weapon. For the last fifteen years, the official doctrine for linking nuclear weapons to European security has been the so-called 'flexible response' employing the 'NATO Triad' of conventional, tactical nuclear and strategic nuclear weapons. The first line of allied resistance to conventional attack is to be conventional resistance; if that fails, tactical nuclear weapons used on the battlefield are both to reinforce the defence and raise the spectre of escalation; finally, if all else fails, nuclear weapons are to be employed more widely and ultimately 'strategically' against the Soviet Union.[5]

This formula reveals NATO's basic dilemma: the fact that the most powerful nuclear forces in the West belong to the United States, while the most likely battlefield belongs to a collection of independent European allies. Clearly the United States has an interest in postponing the moment of strategic nuclear war, which is the only kind that involves American territory, but any plans to prolong the nuclear or even conventional phases of war in Europe may weaken Soviet fears of escalation and would certainly devastate Europe if implemented. President de Gaulle delivered such famous warnings as 'who can say that, if the occasion arises, the two, while each deciding not to launch its missiles at the main enemy, so that it shall itself be spared, will not crush the others?', and went off to play Massive Retaliation by himself.[6] In his memoirs, Dr Kissinger displayed the opposite perspective when he wrote: 'Europeans favoured ... the early use of strategic nuclear weapons, which means a United States–Soviet nuclear war fought over their heads. This was precisely what was unacceptable to American planners.'[7]

The divergence of interests is real but it is, I think, a dangerous oversimplification to characterize it, as some do, as a European preference for *deterrence* and an American preference for *defence*. Everyone in NATO wants deterrence, because any war with nuclear weapons about ≐ indeed any war at all between powerful alliances – would be a dreadfully dangerous business. The argument is about how to do the deterring. In the current debate over theatre nuclear weapons, some unilateralists, ably supported by several Soviet research institutes, suggest a positive American eagerness for a limited nuclear war confined to Europe. The obvious imponderables surrounding such a war, the vulnerability of the immense American garrison and countless American families in Europe, the obvious danger of escalation to the intercontinental level however unintended, make it extremely difficult for me to understand why the United States should run such risks, when the alternative of abandoning Europe to its fate seems much more attractive. Moreover, if Europeans would naturally prefer successful deterrence to war, most of them by no means want an assurance that, if deterrence fails, the resulting war would immediately become nuclear and unrestricted.

Admittedly a few Americans as well as Europeans have advocated that a policy of immediate recourse to nuclear weapons would be the most effective deterrent. Such strategies can range from the old idea of a thin screen of forces as a tripwire to trigger nuclear retaliation on Soviet territory – what is called 'prompt deterrence' these days in the Netherlands – to the proposals for using so-called 'mini-nukes' solely on the battlefield as an adjunct to conventional defence. The truth is, however, that to be credible such policies would require virtually automatic action, perhaps by predelegated authority to military commanders to use nuclear weapons. Years of alliance history have made it quite clear that no government, European or American, is willing to commit itself finally to the use of nuclear weapons until it can see the exact circumstances in which the need arises.[8]

Consequently, NATO strategy contains an inevitable element of uncertainty. This provides endless opportunity for uneasiness and recrimination. Allied statesmen have done their best to make a virtue of this ambiguity. The former British Defence Minister Duncan Sandys once referred to 'an area in-between about which I will not speculate and which I will not define'.[9] Less elegantly but with equally accomplished obfuscation, a recent Director of Nuclear Planning at NATO explained: 'The NATO doctrine for the use of nuclear weapons is clear, concise, simple and direct. It is that, when required, the alliance would respond with nuclear weapons on the scale appropriate to the circumstances.'[10]

In practice there are two different kinds of ambiguity in the strategy. The official one is designed to keep the Soviet Union uncertain about when and how nuclear weapons are to be used, but not about whether they *would* be used. Unofficially, many Europeans are uncertain whether the United States would actually use nuclear weapons on their behalf, but they hope the allegedly smaller risk of using weapons on the battlefield would tempt the United States at least *that* far onto the slippery slope of escalation – and that *that* prospect will deter Soviet aggression in the first place.

The recent trend of the military balance has greatly increased the strain on this creaking hinge in the alliance. Soviet striking power against the United States, authenticated in the SALT treaties, discredits the idea of an American retaliation at the strategic level, while the increased conventional power of the Soviet army compels NATO to rely as much as ever on the threat of escalation. NATO's options are therefore confined more than ever to that intermediate level of nuclear action on the battlefield where its advantage once lay. It has therefore been a natural and politically devastating move for the Soviet Union to turn to building up its capability at precisely this level of nuclear armament.

The great bogey of this Soviet effort is the notorious SS20 – a mobile missile with multiple warheads and a range of some 5,000 kilometres. Over 250 of these have been deployed since 1976 and a new one is now appearing every five days. As a result there has been a 56 per cent increase in the number of Soviet warheads of this intermediate range over the last twelve months. It has been a great mistake, I believe, if an understandable one, for NATO to seize on the SS20 as a convenient excuse to justify refurbishing NATO's own battlefield and theatre nuclear weapons when, as we can see, the problem is really part of the overall decay of NATO's relative capability at this and other levels of warfare. The SS20 is in fact only one part of a whole new family of Soviet nuclear weapons in the European theatre, ranging from another missile of over 1,000-km range down through shorter-range missiles to the introduction of Soviet nuclear artillery, coupled with new nuclear-capable aircraft. These weapons ensure that even if the so-called 'zero-option' were negotiated at the level of the SS20–Cruise missile and Pershing II, a great Soviet nuclear capability would remain and with it Western Europe's vulnerability.[11]

With this much more effective, accurate, controllable array of weapons, the Soviet Union may believe that NATO would not dare use its own battlefield weapons first, because it would be out-fought and because NATO's old plan of escalating to the theatre level, perhaps involving Soviet territory, is now also untenable because of the much-improved Soviet capability to fight at that level also, all without involving the intercontinental weapon. It is thus not the SS20 – though it represents a great leap in military capability over its cruder predecessors – but the overall strategic context within which the theatre nuclear balance has turned against NATO, that constitutes the genuinely new problem confronting the Western alliance.

How can NATO best deal with this problem? I think we must recognize there *is* no wholly satisfactory answer. Once again we feel the other edge of the sword. Our former strategies have not been perfect and nor will their successors be. If this is uncomfortable for residents of Western Europe, it is the price of living next door to an unpleasant superpower.

So long as there *is* a nuclear Soviet Union, Western Europe needs a nuclear deterrent to ensure the Soviet Union never comes to believe it could use or threaten to use its nuclear weapons in Europe with impunity. This requires a retaliatory nuclear capability able to threaten attacks on Soviet territory if the damage in Europe ever reaches intolerable levels. At present there are three main sources of such potential retaliation: first there are the national British and French nuclear forces, which reach their most plausible level of credibility on the assumption that British and French territory is already under attack; secondly, there are the limited strategic options of the United States, discussed in my last lecture and, thirdly, there are attacks launched on the Soviet Union or on Soviet forces in Eastern Europe by American nuclear weapons based in Europe. It is, of course, to reinforce the last possibility that the current modernization programme involving the Cruise missiles and Pershing II has been proposed.

The idea that the threat of such attacks is more plausible if mounted from European territory is well embedded in the strategic literature. Primarily it is argued that credible threats of retaliation call for a certain symmetry and appropriateness – even, if you like, legitimacy – and that this would be observed by retaliation from the actual territory under attack.[12] Using only theatre weapons

39

would also, it is said, signify to the enemy a desire to stop short of the ultimate stages of superpower conflict and a willingness to terminate the war if the immediate aggression in progress is halted. Further deterrent effect may be extracted from the symbolic presence of these American weapons on European soil and the fact that they would be overrun in a successful Soviet invasion.

The Soviet Union, of course, denies it would recognize any such distinctions and asserts it would retaliate directly on the United States if Soviet territory were struck. I have no doubt this is possible and that the Soviet Union does think it unfair that it can be struck by medium-range American forces from Europe, while it can only hit the United States with the long-range systems covered by SALT. But before we are carried away with sympathy we should note the corollary of that belief, which is that the Soviet Union should be able to rain weapons on Western Europe with impunity.

Deterrence is a matter of painstakingly denying an enemy any option that offers him promise of success without disproportionate costs. If NATO had no ability to hit the Soviet Union in a war confined to Europe, it would leave just such a hole in its defences. I conclude that the modernization and strengthening of NATO's capability to fight at this level deserves support. The specific proposal to introduce Cruise missiles and Pershing II, however, seems to me neither so essential nor so dangerous as the extreme advocates on each side of the current bitter controversy suggest. What is important is for Europe to be seen to be working seriously and in harmony with the United States on reinforcing this peculiarly sensitive link in transatlantic relations. This link is needed, SS20 or not, and it is the whole Western nuclear arsenal that needs review and refurbishment, not merely the few weapons embodied in the current controversial package. American willingness to field systems in Europe that can breach those limits that the Soviet Union suggests would mark the onset of intercontinental war seems to me to be as far as the United States can go in registering the unacceptability of a substantial nuclear war confined to Europe and, insofar as they believe what they say about escalation, the Soviet leaders should be much deterred.

But just as we should not be mesmerized by the SS20 into ignoring the wider significance of the theatre nuclear balance, we should not allow the nuclear questions to blind us to the other elements in deterrence. It is the fact that the Soviet Union cannot attack Western Europe without getting into war with the United States that ties American nuclear power most firmly to European security. Moreover, while it is Soviet *nuclear* power that compels NATO to maintain its own nuclear forces in Europe, it is Soviet conventional superiority that compels NATO to consider using the nuclear weapons first. The more credible NATO's conventional capability, the more plausible the rationale for the presence of the American troops and the more postponable become those divisive questions about the nature and timing of nuclear action. Indeed, if the Soviet Union is tempted to believe NATO might never dare use its nuclear weapons, the more urgent the need to reduce Soviet confidence in victory in a wholly conventional war.

Reluctance to redouble efforts at conventional defence arises partly from failure to recognize that, as in the nuclear field, well-considered preparations make the war planned for less and not more likely, and partly from a belief that the task is hopeless anyway. Yet, even while acknowledging that the recent increase in threats on the flanks of NATO and beyond may put added stress on allied forces, a proper application of modern technology even within present budgets offers real prospects of enhanced defensive effectiveness. Some new conventional weapons offer capabilities not much less impressive than the battlefield nuclear weapons. New clusters of individually guided anti-tank bomblets, for example, offer a single aircraft or missile a tank-killing power comparable to the dreaded neutron bomb and with much less political fuss.[13]

Such technology needs to be adapted, with the minimum of preconceived tactical ideas, to the exploitation of all the difficulties the Soviet army would face if it undertook the formidable task of overrunning Europe. I said in the last lecture that enemies had to be deterred in terms of their own strategic doctrines, but defeated according to our own. I should now modify that principle by pointing out that an enemy's doctrine places certain operational requirements upon him, and if those are correctly singled out for attack, he will fail. With its strong belief that success depends on meeting the required norms of material and performance, the Soviet army ought to be very open to deterrence by the skilled identification and exploration of its vulnerabilities.

At the end of this lecture, I return to the deeper political implications of the current strategic debate. The Soviet campaign against the NATO decision to modernize nuclear weapons is a claim to a veto on Western Europe's efforts to manage its own affairs. Given a minimal Western capability for defence and a vestige of credibility in the United States' nuclear guarantee, the greater danger has always been not so much that the Soviet Union would actually attack, as that it would lean increasingly hard on Western European political independence of decision. By reaching deeper into the domestic European political debate about defence, the Soviet Union is groping its way toward what has been its consistent goal since 1945: a decisive voice in the determination of Western Europe's political future and particularly the re-establishment of the recognized status in All-German affairs it briefly enjoyed as an occupying power. This would be a great prize, vindicating Peter the Great as well as Lenin, for the advance would be both strategic and ideological.

To prevent the Soviet Union turning its threatened setback in Eastern Europe into a success in the West, requires a degree of self-confidence in Western Europe that I do not believe can be sustained over time, in crisis as in calm, without a credible balance of military power. Such a balance is also, I believe, the precondition for further hopeful political evolution in Eastern Europe and a successful outcome to efforts to negotiate measures of mutual reassurance. For as I shall argue in a later lecture, sound arms control must be based on sound strategic foundations.

Finally I come to a thought which I fear has little political future at present but which is nevertheless at the heart of the matter. Most of the problems I have been discussing arise from that fault-line between European and American interests. Can Western Europe, wealthy and populous as it is, forever avoid looking more to its own defence and the mutual collaboration that it will require? The present moment seems hardly the time to revive the idea of a European Defence Community. Interestingly though, in a recent opinion poll, just over half of the respondents supported a West European defence policy independent of America, and this was endorsed by almost half of those under 25. Even in these difficult days we see the small but remarkable initiative for a European Community role in the Sinai peacekeeping force. The European Parliament is edging, however gingerly, toward questions of security.[14] Never did the United States have more need of a powerful and self-reliant partner. If a fraction of the enthusiasm and ingenuity mustered in opposition to Western strategy were harnessed to such possibilities it would, I believe, do a great deal more to preserve the peace.

4 The Strategic Dimension of the Third World

The Strategic Dimension of the Third World

Events in the Persian Gulf over the past few years have reminded us how Western Europe's expensive direct investment in its security, which I discussed in my last lecture, could be seriously outflanked by a successful blockade or embargo on oil supplies. The significance of the Middle East for European security used to be symbolized by the overlapping membership of NATO and CENTO, the Central Treaty Organization which evolved from the ill-fated Baghdad Pact. Oil and the much more ancient strategic significance of the Middle East as the meeting place of three continents make this area a keystone of global strategy. Two distinguishable processes are at work there: one, the pursuit of the world's dominating ideological and political power struggle between the East-West camps, led by the United States and the Soviet Union; the other, the painful emergence of a pattern of security relations among the newly fledged states of the area. In this respect, the Middle East is merely the most significant microcosm of an evolution at work throughout the so-called Third World; an evolution that will determine the strategic shape of the world for decades to come.

The European and strategic-nuclear balances I have discussed so far in these lectures are expensive, dangerous and fluid, but, partly for these reasons, they have so far been stable in that there has been little war or change in political alignment in the developed world. It is in the Third World that not only the indigenous nations but also the powers of the developed world have shed most blood since 1945. This is not surprising, for there is nothing to prevent it. The organizing structure of deterrence and confrontation that has stabilized the blocs around the superpowers in the developed world has no parallel in the Third World.

Consequently there has been free rein for the many specific Third World conflicts arising from frontier disputes, from unstable regimes nervous about the domestic rivals harboured by their neighbours, or from economic need and unevenly distributed resources. Perhaps because nationalism has raised the price of open imperialism, the typical goal is not to seize territory as such, but to make and break regimes. Tanzania, for example, did not annex Uganda but installed President Nyerere's friend Obote. In many ways the war of regimes can be more bitter than traditional territorial ambition, for the former tends to be less reversible and more obviously fatal for leaderships. Nevertheless, there are still wars and threats of annexation and partition, as the cases of Belize and Bangladesh illustrate.

The scale of war in the Third World is not usually large and the most common forms are brief, intermittent and sometimes covert. In the Middle East, however, and in the Indo-Pakistani conflicts, a great deal of traditional land, sea and air warfare has occurred, with great consumption of armaments. The burden of these armaments on less developed countries is frequently deplored, and understandably so. Overall figures are misleading, however, for the truly astronomical expenditures, reaching 20–30 per cent of Gross National Product, are confined largely to the Middle East, where the capacity to pay, either from oil revenues or American aid, is high. India, however, spends only some 3 per cent of GNP, or $6–7 per head, and the typical poor country much less.

Public attention often attaches to rash expenditure – or acquisition by gift – of complex equipment beyond the mastery of the local troops. Indonesia, one of the Soviet Union's earliest ventures in arming the Third World, acquired notorious amounts of quickly rusted machinery, and Iran, though the degree of folly there is much more debatable, also aimed very high under the Shah. It is frequently overlooked, however, that a great deal of modern military technology is ideally suited for unskilled and ill-organized armies – hand-held missiles that put great hitting power into a footsoldier's hands, and even more powerful weapons that can be bought off the shelf, pre-packaged and ready for use with no further maintenance. For smaller conflicts this may be sufficient, but the larger wars of the Third World have consumed munitions at a pace that has led the great powers to reassess their own stocks nervously and that, by making the belligerents dependent on immediate re-supply (as was the case on a grand scale in the Middle East war of 1973), dramatized the extent to which the supply of arms creates new dimensions of entanglement and mutual leverage between the developed and less developed worlds.[1]

There is an understandable temptation in the Western democracies to steer clear of the conflicts of the Third World, an area so voracious of assistance, especially at a time when the sparks of distant – and not so distant – conflict could conceivably ignite our own powder-barrels. As we wash our hands, we would doubtless, according to our temperament, regard ourselves as leaving the Third World to stew in its own juice or as respecting the inherent dignity and independence of newly created states. While such abstention may be possible and wise in many particular cases, however, it is not practicable as a universal rule.

For one thing, as we have all been so forcibly reminded recently, the Western industrial community – and in its own less intense manner, the Communist bloc – has vital interests in the markets and raw materials of the Third World. Oil is, of course, the most spectacular if transient example of this, because of its critical economic role, the lack of short-term substitutes and the dominant role of the Gulf area in its supply. The prolonged disruption of oil supplies that could result from malicious acts or mere chaos would produce a catastrophic fall in industrial output. The power to create such interruptions therefore becomes a formidable political weapon and the question of oil supply must consequently be a consideration, if sometimes unspoken, in *any* future confrontations between the West and the Soviet Union, as well as more obviously in crises in the Middle East itself.[2] Oil apart, however, the preservation of a world order open to trade on a commercial basis is a vital Western interest. There is room for argument about the fair terms of such trade, but the Third World nations themselves are in no doubt about their need for access to the world's most advanced economies.

It is not, however, a matter of economics alone; most people in the developed democracies would feel oppressed and claustrophobic if the Third World abandoned its admittedly defective but still pluralistic patterns of government and settled for uniform totalitarianism and command instead of market economies. Our desire

49

to preserve what has been called a 'compatible' world, and the Communist powers' equal eagerness to spread their own system, consequently inject the East–West dimension into the current phase of relations with the Third World.

But there is another feature of the strategic scene in the Third World which compels universal attention without such a clear division in East–West interests. That feature is the prospect of nuclear proliferation, which would introduce a terrifying new element into the turbulence of the Third World.

When Britain became the third nuclear power in the 1950s it was widely expected that many others would rapidly follow suit. Each new nuclear acquisition has aroused similar fears. In fact the progress has been mercifully slow; France, China and India followed Britain at intervals of eight, four and ten years, with Israel, at an unknown date, being generally supposed to have, if not a bomb, then the capability to assemble one in a matter of days. The more recent stages in the diffusion of nuclear power, if slow, have a geographical significance, for they mark the shift of the wave of acquisition from the developed to the less developed world. The developed world's apparatus of blocs and extended deterrence, so frequently deplored, obviously serves a useful purpose so far as proliferation is concerned, for numerous countries which are among the best qualified technologically to make nuclear weapons, like Japan, Italy or Canada, have not felt the need to do so. Consequently, the most likely candidates on most lists of prospective nuclear powers lie outside the major security alignments. Indeed, to prove the point, some of the most worrying candidates are among the isolated so-called pariah states, like South Africa, Taiwan, South Korea and, until recently, Iran.[3]

It is generally assumed that the spread of nuclear weapons is a bad thing. In principle, I agree, though the view is not universal. The French General Pierre Gallois, the most vociferous veteran proponent of the French nuclear force, is often taken as the intellectual leader of those who believe that the proliferation of nuclear weapons will also diffuse the ideas of deterrence and with them the state of relative stalemate that characterizes the balance in Europe.[4] Most people, however, assume life in a nuclear crowd would be dangerous. By definition, many disputes which now have no chance of 'going nuclear', could do so if one or more of the parties possessed nuclear weapons. Many of the particular candidates for nuclear power have characteristics suggesting that, in their case, possession would be closer than is comfortable to actual use, for I have already mentioned the prevalence of armed conflict and political instability in the Third World. A country like Libya with a nuclear weapon is a terrifying thought. New nuclear forces might also be *technically* unsound so far as safety and control are concerned. Moreover the very process of proliferation, in which nuclear forces might be imminent but not operational, could lead to acute 'pre-nuclear' conflicts; a theoretical possibility recently made reality by the Israeli air attack on the Iraqi reactor.

There is also the sobering thought that if small nuclear forces were actually used with results that, perhaps because of their very smallness, proved not to be utterly catastrophic, the useful taboo on nuclear war that has been observed since Nagasaki might be broken, with unpredictable consequences for the climate of restraint elsewhere. Thus beyond the obvious ecological dangers to the whole world from nuclear explosions in the atmosphere, there are implications of Third World proliferation for the balance between the longer-established nuclear powers. Already the Soviet Union claims credit in the SALT negotiations for its need to take account of French, British, and – though less is said in public – Chinese nuclear strength. Most of the homelands of the developed countries lie beyond the likely initial capability to deliver weapons from the less developed countries, but the Middle East and Europe are not far apart and there are, at least in theory, many clandestine or unorthodox ways to launch a purely terroristic attack. New nuclear forces must thus of necessity compel existing nuclear powers to review their own requirements – anti-missile defence, for example, makes better sense against small nuclear forces than large, and it was precisely against China's embryonic forces that the United States somewhat insincerely justified its first venture in that direction. Moreover states with the capability to make nuclear weapons but which have hitherto resisted might reconsider on grounds of both prestige and security if new and perhaps otherwise humble members joined the nuclear club. Some nations form especially significant junction points on the pattern of proliferation and do so in more than one frame of reference: India's nuclear test, for example, stimulated responses not merely in its neighbour, Pakistan, but also, by its demonstration of Asian achievement, in Taiwan and Korea.

There are thus general as well as particular dangers in nuclear proliferation. This does not mean there is a simple correlation between increased numbers of nuclear powers and increased danger. It matters a great deal who gets nuclear weapons, when and how. A nuclear force *could* be the stabilizing factor in a military balance. I doubt if all my listeners would deplore the news, if they had it confirmed, that Israel *does* have a nuclear capability and that the Arabs believe it.[5] I made clear in the last lecture my belief that it would be damaging rather than helpful for the British and French to abandon their existing nuclear forces. But I do not see why possession by a few need necessarily become universal. It has not happened for many years now among many nations well able to do the trick technically. At no period of history, I think, have all military powers wanted or been able to possess all the most powerful weapons of their time. Nevertheless the *general* dangers of proliferation are such that I think the burden of proof is on anyone who wants to encourage a new power to join the nuclear ranks, and I believe therefore that a non-proliferation policy is wise.

So how is such a policy to be implemented? It used to be thought the secret was to stop nations gaining the technical ability to make nuclear weapons, especially by denying them probably the most difficult stage, the manufacture and separation of the fissile materials, plutonium-239 and uranium-235. Now, both the Non-Proliferation Treaty – the NPT – and the IAEA, the International Atomic Energy Authority, are meant to serve this purpose by combining pledges against making or transferring nuclear weapons with the supervision of nuclear materials. Ironically, however, the price exacted by non-nuclear powers for accepting this restrictive system was the promise that the nuclear powers and the International Atomic Energy Authority would encourage and facilitate – almost sanctify, it seems at times – the spread of peaceful nuclear technology. This has been so successful that literally dozens of nations will soon have on their territory fissile material in various stages of refinement, most of it in their own legal ownership, and which they are forbidden from adapting to military uses only by bilateral agreements and by the Non-Proliferation Treaty itself, from which they may legally withdraw at three months' notice. My friend Albert Wohlstetter, the American strategic analyst and father of the phrase 'the delicate balance of terror', likes to quote the unlikely authority of Florence Nightingale at this point, when she commented tartly that 'Whatever else hospitals do, they shouldn't spread disease.'

Now I do not think this means we could have a much better non-proliferation treaty, for I believe that economic pressures will inexorably spread nuclear technology for peaceful purposes. We can strengthen the technical barriers and make life difficult for the less capable would-be nuclear powers, but denying the physical capacity to make bombs seems a wasting asset in the non-proliferation effort. Prohibition can serve as a warning system and warning can be made use of; but I think that the way to make use of it, and the key to the whole problem, is to work tirelessly and pragmatically on reinforcing each candidate's disincentive to proceed.

The incentives and disincentives to acquire a military capability are many. Prestige plays a role as an incentive and expense as a disincentive. But the most powerful considerations naturally arise from the strategic balance itself. Thus if the great powers of the developed world are to discourage nuclear proliferation in the Third World, they will have to play a role in the security affairs of that world. This already happens, of course. When both South Korea and Taiwan reacted to the Indian nuclear test and the weakening of American prestige following Vietnam, by moving toward nuclear reprocessing, the United States not only twisted their economic arms to desist but strengthened its security assurances on the clear condition that the nuclear efforts subsided. President Carter's plan to withdraw the American garrison from South Korea was shelved.

Guarantees, however, are frequently unacceptable to Third World countries, at least if they are overt, for reasons of self-esteem and local political alignment. Sometimes the great powers can serve the same purpose by supplying the wherewithal for aspiring nuclear powers to meet their security needs with conventional arms. Arms supplies to Israel are commonly described as an inducement for Israel to keep its bomb in the basement, and recently military aid to Pakistan has obviously been related to an effort – abortive perhaps – to persuade Pakistan not to follow India's example and test a nuclear 'device'.

An ironic conclusion from all this is that the much-denigrated arms trade may be playing an essential role in curbing proliferation.[6] Similarly, the pledge to reduce their own nuclear armament, put in the Non-Proliferation Treaty as a price for getting the non-nuclear powers to accept such an inherently discriminatory contract, the pledge frequently referred to as curbing 'vertical' as well as 'horizontal' proliferation, may be counter-productive. For only a powerful and self-confident superpower could, for instance, serve as the guarantor to relieve Israel of the need to plan its own nuclear deterrent against Soviet intervention or reassure Egypt and Israel against each other's nuclear potential.

The proliferation issue thus brings me back to where I started this lecture, the fact that armed conflict is endemic in the Third World and likely to remain so, and that the great powers, certainly the two superpowers, are inextricably entangled in this system. If the great powers are to discourage proliferation by manipulating the power balance in the Third World as best they can, their task is complicated by the fact that it has to be performed in the context of the other security problems besetting the Third World and by the great powers' own divergent interests there.

Looked at from a primarily military perspective, there has been a marked and peculiar reversal in the behaviour of the two super-powers and their allies over the past decade or so. In the 1960s, the European colonial powers were rounding off the wars of imperial retreat in such campaigns as the British 'confrontation' with In-donesia on behalf of the new Malaysia, while the United States, inspired by the theories of counter-insurgency, entered South-east Asian wars under the banner of containing communism and ended up in the Vietnamese disaster. Both Anglo-Saxon powers derived a serious dose of disillusionment from these experiences and both withdrew with a remarkably similar rhetoric of 'never again'. In various mixtures, the rationale of retreat embraced the conclusions that the interests at stake had not been so important after all, that they could be pursued by politico-economic means – with com-forting sentiments such as the 'Arabs can't drink the oil' – and that if the Soviet Union tried to follow where Western imperialists once trod, they would find the locals equally recalcitrant; moreover if the West did want to intervene in Third World balances, it could do so by backing up local clients from a safe distance.[7]

Now the Soviet Union, for its part, has sought ever since its foundation to extend its influence over the less developed as well as developed world. This has been partly an ideological imperative and partly a result of the Soviet obsession – inherited from Russia and compounded by Bolshevik revolutionary experience – with real and imagined external threats. It has been ironically observed that the Soviet Union feels encircled because the world is round and that they think it a fortunate feature of solid geometry that after they control half the globe, each further addition to their territory will reduce the length of their exposed frontier!

Until recently, however, the Soviet Union has lacked the capacity to project its own military power directly beyond its immediate vicinity. Starting in the mid-fifties with the energetic arming of Nasser's Egypt and Mr Khrushchev's assertion that wars of national liberation were certainly not to be included in his newly enunciated principle that war was no longer a necessary contingency in the struggle against capitalism under nuclear conditions, the Soviet Union has increasingly provided itself with means of military action at a distance. The expansion of the Soviet navy has been much publicized; the development of a large strategic airlift and the maintenance of seven airborne divisions less so.[8]

Of course, all of these forces have roles in a potential European or Chinese war. But as the rhetoric of retreat has sounded around Western Third World strategy in the last decade, that of advance has emerged louder and louder in the Soviet Union. Rendered more confident by nuclear parity, which confers what one might call a degree of 'undeterrence', Soviet leaders have frankly declared that the improved correlation of forces frees them to act more boldly overseas. Thus in 1980, to give an example, Mr Mikhail Suslov, the Kremlin's senior ideologue, observed that 'the change in the correlation of forces in favour of Socialism has created favourable conditions for the growth of the people's liberation struggle. Major victories,' he said, 'have been won in recent years by the forces of national liberation and social progress in the countries of Asia, Africa and Latin-America.'[9] As Marshal Grechko, the former Soviet Minister of Defence, had made clear in an earlier speech, the Soviet role includes direct military action: 'At the present stage,' he stated, 'the historic function of the Soviet Armed Forces is not restricted merely to their function in defending our Motherland and other socialist countries. In its foreign policy activity, the Soviet state actively, purposefully opposes the export of counter-revolution and the policy of oppression, supports the national liberation struggle, and resolutely resists imperialist aggression in whatever distant region of our planet it may appear.'[10]

Put into practice, we have seen a clear shift from the covert and oblique to the direct and open style of Soviet military action in the Third World, limited though it still is. Soviet pilots flew air cover over Cairo in 1970, a notable innovation; the brilliant use of Cuban forces in Angola and Ethiopia kept the Soviet military role down somewhat, but the Afghan affair has marked a clear increase in scale.

Afghanistan may need cautious interpretation as an indication of Soviet intentions because it is both in the Third World and contiguous to the Soviet border. Nevertheless, it does not seem unduly alarmist to conclude that, where practicable, Soviet forces may henceforth be used directly to prevent reversal of the successes of Soviet-inspired regimes in the Third World as they have repeatedly been used in Eastern Europe. Until Afghanistan, at least, these interventions have been genuinely welcomed by such Soviet protégés as in Ethiopia and Angola; for if the Soviet Union has little to offer these days by way of economic and social example, it is undoubtedly expert in the widely demanded art of seizing and holding power. Nor, the Soviet Union has made perfectly plain, does détente or an understanding at the level of nuclear arms control, imply, as Dr Kissinger seems to have hoped, any lessening of such overseas activism; indeed it seems probable the Soviet Union sees such understandings as registering its achievement of status as a truly world power, and regards the hostile Western reaction as an unjustified attempt to put back the clock.[11]

Even before the Iranian revolution and Afghan invasion aroused acute anxiety about the Persian Gulf, the Soviet and Cuban forays into Africa had stimulated second thoughts in the West about the wisdom of forswearing a military role in the Third World. With the so-called Carter doctrine of resisting aggression in the Middle East, the Rapid Deployment Force, the forward basing of AWACS aircraft and the familiar search for bases and facilities, the United States is reversing its retreat and calling its allies to join it in the troubled waters. But for a variety of reasons, some more honourable than others, the response has been less than overwhelming.

It would be presumptuous and foolhardy for me to prescribe solutions. It may not be so reckless to utter a few cautions and to suggest some things that should *not* be done. Someone has very well said – I only wish I could remember who, but I think it was in French – that we imagine the past and remember the future. We should certainly not imagine we can recreate some golden age of

Western control over Third World affairs. Soviet capability for 'power projection', as it is called, will not disappear. Nor can the Third World countries be treated as the mere objects of policy now they have tasted autonomy, acquired a great deal of military power, and demonstrated to Communist and capitalist alike the costs of taking on an Afro-Asian guerrilla war.

This suggests to me that the underlying idea of the post-Vietnam American strategy, of operating as much as possible through the local structures of power, was sound, if inadequate by itself. Here and there, signs of regional stabilization are appearing in the Third World, through the emergence of a pre-eminent regional power, like Nigeria or Brazil – or, critics may say, like Iran. There are also embryonic regional organizations such as the Organization of African Unity or the Association of South East Asian Nations which embody a useful idea of mutual restraint. If the West is to be true to its professed ideal of national independence it will encourage such developments.

The cheapest way to do so, in both political and economic terms, is by diplomatic and economic action, rather than military. But when Cuban, Libyan and even Soviet forces can be called in to affect the issue, elements friendly to the West clearly need confidence in some countervailing power. A vast amount of recent research shows that though long-term political stability has rarely been achieved by Western military intervention alone, it has often been the precondition for successful later political evolution. For that reason, however, it is necessary to be selective, and the wider struggle with the Soviet Union entails the danger of intervention in places where the conditions for success do not exist, merely because the Soviet hand is thought to have been seen. We cannot completely control the incidence of crises; we can, however, ensure that our response is tailored to each occasion on its merits.

Despite the dramatic growth of Soviet capability for projecting military power, an alliance led by the United States remains well equipped to compete. American logistic facilities still exceed those of the Soviet Union for most areas of the globe and recent measures will enhance them. But logistic capability measured in conventional terms is not wholly relevant in a competition where he who is first on the spot is rarely challenged by the other superpower. The preferred Soviet use of armed force has been to protect the gains of prior political and subversive action. Quick decision and rapid action is therefore at least as valuable as crude fighting power. This is a field where much modern technology can ease the difficulties of the decision-maker, providing the very idea of intervention is not anathema to domestic public opinion. In this respect it may be hopeful to note that it is failure rather than effort that has caused the sharpest opposition in Western societies.

The one area where the West does not enjoy logistical advantage is the Persian Gulf, with its vast stakes of oil and geopolitics. Geopolitics may, indeed, be more important in the long run, in the game of mutual encirclement which the Soviet-Chinese-American contest involves. Here the myriad of security problems typical of the Third World is compounded by the real possibility of a massive invasion by the Soviet Union. Obviously the ultimate military deterrent to this can only be provided by the United States. Many of the strategic considerations will be well known to you all from extensive public debate. But perhaps I can illustrate the American logistical problem merely by pointing out that Tehran is as close to Dublin as it is to the new Anglo-American Indian Ocean base at Diego Garcia in the Indian Ocean.

Nevertheless the task is far from hopeless. The more imminent dangers arise from local unrest, and this is as amenable to limited measures of economic and military assistance as in any other region. While Soviet capability for an all-out East-West war in the region is vastly superior, its task would by no means be easy. More to the point, it is highly unlikely the Soviet Union wants an all-out war in the region and the task therefore becomes one of creating a sufficiently strong Western presence to make such a prospect possible.[12]

This task brings me back, finally, to the American request that Western Europe and Japan reconsider their military abstention from Third World affairs. America's allies are understandably nervous. They fear the costs of a military role: costs that would be both economic, military and, if the Soviet Union took reprisals, at best expensive in terms of the so-called dividends of détente in Europe and, at worst, raising the danger of a conflict spreading to Europe itself. Many Europeans also doubt the appropriateness of the American prescription for the Third World and cling to the hope and belief that military intervention is neither necessary nor efficacious. Nevertheless, Europe is inevitably involved, not merely because the stakes, particularly oil, affect it but because, in a European nightmare recurrent ever since the Korean War, the forces the

United States needs elsewhere may be bled from its European garrison. Never will the Europeans miss those forces more than when some Third World crisis both draws them away and raises the tension in Europe itself.

But anyone who meets this problem with a plea for a return to the good old days of interallied solidarity, is again imagining the past. Conflict East of Suez has traditionally brought out the worst in the alliance, with Americans denouncing European colonialism and Europeans condemning American militarism. Remember the Suez crisis itself.

If we are to master the problem today and in the future, then I think both sides will have to yield a little. So long as the Europeans – and the Japanese – acknowledge that the problem exists, the choice lies between the added effect created by united allied action, sharing the risks and political costs, and the benefits of allies acting separately, each exploiting its own special contacts and relationships. The fact that much of the most effective action called for is political and economic or, if military, at a low level, all this makes a case for continued independence of action. Certainly the United States needs the powerful European and Japanese economies mobilized to sustain friendly regimes in the Third World. But when it comes to military action, the new-found reach of Soviet forces can only be convincingly offset by the United States. Underneath such an umbrella, however, it may be that the small but experienced forces of Britain and France can do continued useful work. Somewhat surprisingly, in the BBC opinion poll I cited in my last lecture, more than half, including half of those under 25 and almost half of Labour-voters, were willing to see Britain play a military role in the Middle East again if British interests were threatened, while only under one-third were opposed. In the longer run, Western Europe and Japan will have to consider whether it is possible to exercise worldwide economic and political power on a grand scale without any matching military capability. I do not expect a quick answer to the question, because however the contemporary East-West contest works out, generations may pass before the process of adding dozens of new nations to the world power balance has run its course.

5 The Limitations of Arms Control

The Limitations of
Arms Control

As I turn to look at arms control and disarmament only in this, my fifth lecture, you may think I have left the horse well behind the cart. Many people today clearly believe that a discussion of armed force should consist chiefly of vehemently advocating disarmament. It is easy and popular to do this, especially if you pass lightly over the difficulties. But as arms control is intended to avert some of the dangers presented by our strategic environment, it seemed reasonable to give that some examination before evaluating the cures prescribed. In a climate of shrill exhortation some notes of caution may not come amiss. Uncritical enthusiasm may actually obscure the very real if limited benefits that the idea of arms control may yield. For in the nuclear age some element of control we must certainly have.

Arms control is a vast subject, irresistible to thesis writer and pamphleteer alike. Even the bibliographies cover whole shelves.[1] Rather than devote this brief lecture to a breathless survey, I will try to single out a few aspects that illuminate both the limitations and the potential of arms control.

The terms 'disarmament' and 'arms control' are commonly used interchangeably, but as I pointed out in my first lecture, there are really two fundamentally different theories. Indeed when the United States Arms Control and Disarmament Agency was founded in 1961 there was a major congressional battle over which order the terms should take in the Agency's title.

The simpler idea, though the more radical and elusive aim, is that of disarmament, by which is usually meant reduction in the quantity, and perhaps even total abolition, of armaments. This approach has most plausibility if you believe armaments are the primary, perhaps even the sole, source of international conflict. Then the process of reducing arms would become self-reinforcing and the vicious circle that is widely supposed to exist in the form of an arms race would be reversed in the virtuous direction of growing mutual confidence. It is not I think true, that, as is sometimes argued, arms are merely a *symptom* and never a *cause* of conflict, so that wherever disarmament is possible, it is not really needed. For military issues *can* be a source of tension. But without my delivering a course of lectures on the theory of international politics, I imagine most of us can intuitively agree that arms are not the *sole* source of conflict. Even a crude historical survey suggests that political events do much more to determine the rate of arms procurement than the interaction of military preparations themselves. Thus it took the invasion of South Korea in 1950 to promote a wave of American rearmament when the Soviet acquisition of nuclear weapons the year before had failed to do so; it was Mr Khrushchev's reopening of the Berlin issue that inspired the surge of rearmament under President Kennedy, the Soviet invasion of Czechoslovakia in 1968 that delayed the start of SALT and thereby probably allowed the development of multiple warheads to get beyond recall, and more recently it was events in the Horn of Africa and Afghanistan that stimulated the American military revival begun by President Carter and continued by President Reagan. On the Soviet side, the great military build-up that still continues was inspired by humiliation in the Cuban missile crisis and by the break with China, rather than by the deployment of American nuclear weapons that had occurred in the 1950s.

If disarmament itself cannot be relied upon to eliminate conflict and as, in any case, armed force cannot be made to disappear in an instant, a framework of security must be maintained, at least during the process of disarmament itself. In the absence of a world government to enforce order, adjudicate disputes and enact peaceful change, this security framework would have to take the continued form of a balance of power. Thus the famous McCloy–Zorin agreement of 1961, which laid down general principles for disarmament, and which is still supposed to govern negotiations between the Soviet Union and the United States, declares that all measures 'should be balanced so that at no stage ... could any state or group of states gain military advantage and that security is ensured equally for all.'[2]

64

These are extremely demanding criteria, even assuming a high degree of goodwill. The modern strategic scene is immensely complex, exhibiting a bewildering array of armament, the significance of which can be judged only within an even more complicated geopolitical context. Even if a theoretically equitable and stable balance *could* be struck, there would remain the task of ensuring that it was established and observed. Faced with a particularly sweeping Russian disarmament proposal, a senior Western statesman once remarked on 'the difficulty of obtaining any true information from Russia and thus the uncertainty of any reciprocity of confidence'. The problem of 'verification', on which Metternich thus put his finger, remains one of the more intractable and one that has only partially been eased by modern technology.

As I mentioned briefly in my first lecture, the difficulty of phasing partial disarmament gave rise in the 1950s to suggestions that a dash should be made for general and complete disarmament within a very few years. This, it was thought, would eliminate the problem of balance and reduce that of verification, for it was said to be easy to tell the difference between 'some' and 'none'.

The reasons why this solution is quite impracticable throw an instructive light on less radical proposals. Complete disarmament is incompatible with the maintenance of domestic order. Even the Covenant of the League of Nations looked only for reductions of arms to a level 'compatible with national safety'; yet the forces needed to maintain law and order in a country like India would have no small capability against India's neighbours. Moreover, far from relaxing, the standards of verification would tighten, because total disarmament would magnify the significance of any weapons that were concealed, especially if they were nuclear. Indeed, many civilian devices, such as aircraft or a pesticide factory that could turn to chemical warfare, would become serious potential instruments of coercion. Starting from such a basis or in more orthodox ways, rearmament would always be possible, and the resulting instabilities would perhaps be greater than those of a fully armed world. The American Civil War, one of the most destructive and the most technologically advanced of its day, began between belligerents virtually disarmed by contemporary European standards. In the current Lebanese civil war, the combatants, many of them amateurs and all with simple weapons, have inflicted more casualties than the last two Arab-Israeli wars put together. In a disarmed world, therefore, it would be only prudent to prepare for a possible breakdown of the system. Yet such preparations would obviously inhibit the development of mutual confidence.

At the end of the fifties, the new concept of 'arms control' emerged in reaction to the sterile hypocrisy of the propaganda battle between grandiose schemes for general disarmament. Arms control shares many of the aims of disarmament, but the underlying assumption and the means envisaged are very different. Arms control is commonly said to seek a reduction in the incidence of war, the mitigation of its effects if it occurs, and to do so if possible at reduced economic cost. But arms control does not assume the resolution of international conflict or the complete elimination of arms. It seeks to steer the military system into safer, cheaper channels, not abolish it, accepting that states will continue to give priority to their own security and to base it on efforts at their own self-defence within a balance of power.

To some extent the aims of arms control are the goals of any rational security policy: even states that go to war are glad to minimize their costs. The insight of arms control is that those costs, whether in war or armed peace, arise from the actions of the enemy; that *he* wants to limit *his* costs, and that he may, therefore, moderate his behaviour if you do likewise. There may indeed be a common interest in moderation even between adversaries. Arms control is thus a *perspective* from which opportunities for mutual restraint may be discerned. Arms control *agreements*, tacit or explicit, are intended to provide reassurance that moderation will be exercised and make plain what the elements in the bargain are. It is important to notice, however, that the incentive to moderate behaviour, and the guarantee that this will be forthcoming, arise from the balance of power and not from the agreements. Thus arms control is a manifestation of deterrence and, like deterrence, actually depends for its success on the very armed force that it is trying to control. It is therefore essential that policies adopted in the name of arms control do not upset the underlying equilibrium.

Arms control is commonly thought of as a process of negotiating agreed limitations between states. But arms control can be pursued unilaterally. Raising the idea of arms control to prominence in strategic thought has provided a constant reminder of the two-edged nature of armed force, and established the importance of not needlessly provoking dangerous reactions in the behaviour of others. Armed forces and weapons can be designed and deployed so as to curb unauthorized, unintended or indiscriminate effects. Weapons can be made as invulnerable as possible so as to minimize enemy temptation to attack them and consequently reduce one's own impulse to precipitate use. The record of recent years suggests that far more has been achieved in such ways, especially where strategic nuclear weapons are concerned, than by negotiated arms-control agreements. There is, indeed, a danger that simplistic notions of arms control, with a bias against anything that cannot be caught in a formal, verifiable, international agreement, may hinder potential contributions to arms control by unilateral measures. Thus, without pausing to settle the issue now, it could be argued that a simple mobile ICBM, though perhaps incompatible with SALT, would have solved the American vulnerability problem more securely and more cheaply than the enormously complicated and expensive MX missile system, and that Cruise missiles, unsuited to first strikes because of their slowness, have not been fully exploited because of the anticipated difficulty of verification.

Of course, the arms-control perspective does not always receive due weight in military planning. Military planners are no more immune than disarmament enthusiasts to tunnel vision, giving their immediate project undue prominence in the wider picture. It was therefore a natural move in bureaucratic politics, as well as a public-relations gesture, for some governments to establish separate arms-control agencies to ensure that this aspect received due attention. Typically, this was carried to the nth degree in the United States, where every new weapon development proposal requires a parallel 'arms control impact' statement. Yet in principle this is a retrograde step, tending to identify arms control as an alien force from outside the military establishment. Properly considered, arms control is not an alternative to defence policy but a criterion by which the latter is to be judged. Indeed it is as an organic element of restraint within defence policy rather than as the subject of international treaties that arms control can probably contribute most to international security.

Nevertheless it is on negotiated agreements that most advocates of arms control seem to pin their hopes. The search for such agreements is necessarily an arduous task, for by definition it is pursued between adversaries or potential adversaries. As I said earlier, agreements can only register balances that the parties are willing to maintain and live with, and the process of negotiation compels them to examine their situation with renewed minuteness and rigour. It is for that reason more than any other that some of the most readily achieved agreements have concerned areas of military competition, such as Antarctica or the seabed, which no party has yet begun seriously exploiting. More generally, it is noticeable that agreements tend to set the seal on existing balances rather than establishing new relations at a lower level.

The mere existence of arms-control negotiations or agreements can certainly not be taken to indicate an underlying harmony of interests, although there are many who would like to think otherwise. The Soviet Union wages an unceasing propaganda campaign employing a stream of arms-control proposals and intensive exploitation of well-meaning disarmament lobbies in the West. But in the more esoteric utterances of their political and military journals, Soviet authorities are refreshingly frank about the nature of the arms-control business.

For them, arms control, like peaceful co-existence, is a modified form of struggle, not a road to reconciliation. Certainly, Soviet leaders accept the need to avoid nuclear war if possible, so that they value the contribution made to crisis management by arms control. They also use arms-control negotiations to inhibit Western military programmes. They give no signs of sharing the view, prevalent in many Western quarters, that their *own* military activities may be dangerous. The Soviet Union is frequently accused of having used the years since the conclusion of the first SALT Treaty in 1972, years of relative lull in American nuclear procurement, to acquire the largest increment of military and especially nuclear power since the Cold War began. This is in no way incompatible with Soviet notions of arms control, however, for arms-control agreements are seen as concessions wrung out of the West by the growth of Soviet power. It is not, as the Russians say, for the sake of their blue eyes that we make agreements with them, but because they leave us no choice. In the words of a leading Soviet writer on arms control, O. V. Bogdanov, 'Life has already shown that imperialism proceeds to measures of disarmament only under the pressure of direct necessity.' Increased Soviet military power, far from endangering arms control, is actually a precondition for it. To quote Georgi Arbatov, head of the Moscow Institute for the Study of the USA, and a recently appointed member of the Central Committee, any 'change in the relationship of forces in favour of the Soviet Union would serve to strengthen peace and international security'.[3] It is therefore also fully in keeping with that candid Soviet view that every opportunity for advantage is taken within an arms-control agreement. This disposition has led to several accusations that the Soviet Union has 'cheated' under the terms of the SALT treaties. Careful examination nearly always reveals however that the so-called cheating is exploitation of the letter of an agreement contrary to what Western governments would like to regard as the spirit.

I do not deny for a minute that Western arms-control negotiators also try to strike bargains favourable to themselves, but I am sure they do not approach their work so consistently as a form of struggle. Still less do I believe that Western public opinion appreciates the gladiatorial nature of the arms-control business.

In such an atmosphere, arms-control negotiations are often intended to achieve results quite different from their ostensible purpose. A negotiating proposal may be seriously intended as a basis for agreement, a gambit on the way to such an agreement or a specious move in quite another game.

To take an example given topical relevance since I prepared this lecture by the grounding of the Soviet Whisky-class submarine in Swedish waters, the Soviet proposal for a Nordic nuclear-free zone would do little to preserve the Scandinavians from nuclear destruction if either superpower wanted to destroy them, but the mere proposal, let alone an agreement, is calculated to widen the divide between the always slightly tentative Nordic members of NATO and their allies. In exactly the same spirit, the Norwegians have cleverly turned the shaft by offering to discuss it provided the area for denuclearization includes the Kola peninsula, which, with Murmansk, includes perhaps the densest single area of Soviet nuclear basing.

A more complex and important example is afforded by the ill-fated Mutual Balanced Force Reduction negotiations in Europe that began in January 1973. To many, I am sure, it seems incomprehensible that such a good idea as reducing the level of armaments in Central Europe should have got nowhere in eight years of arduous talking. In reality, the whole affair is a strategists' and arms controllers' nightmare that becomes much less mysterious if you reflect on the participants' true motives.[4]

NATO entered the talks partly because Soviet pressure for a

conference on security in Europe – the ultimate Helsinki conference – threatened to become a propaganda success for the Russians with no real bearing on security. NATO therefore demanded parallel military talks and the Soviet Union agreed in order to get the Western powers to Helsinki. NATO was also impelled by the efforts of Senator Mansfield to secure substantial withdrawals of American troops from Europe because of West European refusal to shoulder more of the defence burden. Opening negotiations with the Soviet Union enabled the United States government to claim that implementing Senator Mansfield's proposals would throw away American bargaining power. For its part, the Soviet Union cast its proposals in terms of national, not alliance-wide, ceilings on remaining forces. This implied a specific ceiling on the Bundes-wehr and thus served the constant Soviet purpose of isolating the Federal Republic – the danger that in more recent days has made Chancellor Schmidt refuse to take the new theatre nuclear weapons unless at least one Continental ally does so too.

Leaving tangential political purposes on one side and concen-trating solely on the arms-control agenda of the force-reduction talks, we can see the difficulty of trying to adjust or establish a balance of power, rather than merely registering one. As I reminded you in my third lecture, so far as anyone can calculate, the Soviet army enjoys superiority in Central Europe, and the Soviet Union uses this regularly as a way of bringing political pressure to bear. The erosion of NATO's erstwhile superiority in tactical nuclear weapons having trumped one of the West's few bargaining cards, it becomes difficult to see why the Soviet Union should grant NATO the security and equality it will not purchase by its own efforts.

Even if the basis for a deal existed, however, these negotiations also illustrate the technical complexity of the problem. The SALT agreements, widely seen as a masterpiece of diplomacy, chiefly entailed calculating the balance of a few, highly comparable, mis-siles. Striking a balance on the Central Front involves a myriad of land and air weapons, all varying in significance according to terrain, weather, skill of commanders, degree of alertness and the responsiveness of political leaders to strategic warning. From recent history – the German breakthrough in 1940, Israel's campaigns, the American defeat in Vietnam – we know that the number and even quality of men and weapons are far from decisive when what the Russians call operational factors are added in.

Nothing has done more than the SALT treaties, I suppose, to spread the impression we have entered a brave new world of negotiated disarmament. Yet those too, I fear, illustrate the intractability of armed force to control by formal agreement. In the first place, the actual achievement is limited, encouraging the jibe that they are agreements not to do what nobody wanted to do in the first place. The keen disarmer notes that except for a marginal reduction in nuclear delivery vehicles required of the Russians by the unratified second SALT treaty, no actual disarmament is involved at all, unless you count the abstention from anti-ballistic missile defences. Indeed the price paid to secure consent to the agreements within each superpower has probably stimulated strategic procurement. Effort has poured into whatever areas of technology remain unrestricted. The decade since the first SALT treaty has seen the biggest-ever expansion and diversification of Soviet strategic forces; certainly the potential for mutual annihilation still exists.[5]

The SALT agreements provide a good illustration of how the diplomatic need for simple concepts such as parity in one or two dimensions, does violence to the intricacy of the actual strategic problems. The treaties were made possible by the development of satellite-borne and other methods of reconnaissance – the so-called 'national technical means', in the terms of the treaties – that dispensed with the intrusive 'on-site' methods of inspection to which the Soviet Union had always objected. Wonderful though they are, however, these systems have their limitations. Consequently the treaties count not the missiles themselves but the launchers: that is, the emplacements or silos. From this derives the recent American anxiety that the Soviet Union, quite legally under the letter of the treaty, might have a supply of extra missiles as 'reloads'. Contrariwise, the vast expense of the American MX system is largely determined by the need to keep it compatible with verification. The SS20, the Backfire bomber, the Cruise missile and other so-called 'grey area systems' have been largely omitted from the SALT process both because of their elusive technical characteristics and their entanglement with regional powers and balances.

These difficulties seem far more serious to me than the complaints of American hawks that the United States received a bad deal in the treaties. Despite a few biases in favour of the Soviet

Union, as in its unique quota of 'heavy' missiles, nothing in the treaties prevents the United States maintaining a better strategic balance if it has the will to do so. More worrying is the possibility that the complexities of the balance are outstripping the techniques of negotiated control. Perhaps the SALT treaties were a fluke. When negotiations began, *Pravda* wrote that it was 'one of those rare moments in history when both sides are ready to admit equality in the broadest sense and to view this as an initial position for reaching agreement.'[6] We now see that the moment may have been rarer than we thought; not the start of an era but a passing occasion when divergent interests coincided just enough for a 'one-off' deal.

Entering into over-simplified agreements about particular aspects of a complex strategic environment, where politics and technology interact in ever-changing patterns, entails the danger of losing the flexibility with which to adapt to change. The prejudice against technological innovation, especially Western innovation, to which I referred earlier, offers a more generalized illustration of this danger. This prejudice is turning Western defence policy into a series of running fights over whatever is designated 'rogue weapon' of the moment by the disarmament lobby or by Soviet diplomacy. Ironically, secrecy spares the Soviet Union such scrutiny. Soviet systems, often innovations themselves, as in the contemporary example of anti-satellite technology, turn up as *faits accomplis*.

It is difficult to think of any other area of modern life in which so many people assume that today's technology is the best imaginable. In reality much military innovation is devoted to making weapons safer to handle and more amenable to control. Recent American nuclear tests, for example, have perfected new detonating components so that accidents with weapons will be even less likely than at present. A complete test ban would have prevented this development. It is not axiomatic, therefore, that that much-heralded arms-control proposal would be an unquestionable step toward a safer world. Indeed a complete test ban strikes me as a particularly over-confident proposal for freezing a critical part of the military environment without any real knowledge of what the long-term effects would be[7]; while confidence in it as an anti-proliferation measure is limited by the fact that many likely candidates for nuclear status have refused to sign even the present partial ban.

The rigidity you legislate today may deny you the evasive man-
œuvre you want to take tomorrow. In my view, therefore, the
burden of proof is at least as much on those who propose curbs on
technology as on those who sponsor innovations. In reality, I feel
sure the effort to freeze technology is doomed to failure – I can
quote no less an authority than the late Marshal Grechko, former
Soviet Defence Minister, to this effect: 'Today it is impossible to
stand still. A characteristic of our time is the stormy process of
development, renewal and improvement in all spheres of human
activity, among them military affairs.'[8] The Marshal was, of course,
a military man. But in its Yearbook for 1981, even the Stockholm
International Peace Research Institute rejects the idea that man is
being carried along on an irresistible tide of technology. Technology, says the Institute, cannot be saddled with the blame for a
military competition that is really driven by political forces.

A final example of an area of strategic interaction where arms-
control proposals proliferate without much apparent analysis of the
underlying complexities, is that *bête noire* of the would-be reformer,
the arms trade with the Third World. In what we may call his
unreconstructed period, President Carter tirelessly denounced the
'threat to world peace embodied in this spiralling arms traffic'.[9] I
pointed out in an earlier lecture that there is no proven correlation
between the incidence of warfare and the level of armament – it
would be perhaps too cheap a debating point to suggest that if the
theory were absolutely reliable most recent wars ought to have
taken place in Europe. Nor, in fact, is the trade spiralling. That
1981 SIPRI *Yearbook* records a fall in Third World arms imports
since 1975. I could go on to repeat that the Middle East, which
takes 48 per cent of Third World arms imports, has special facilities
for paying, that resources spent on arms would not automatically
be diverted to economic development, and that in many Third
World countries the armed forces are the primary source of order
and even of development.[10]

But my purpose is not to advocate poor nations spending money
on weapons. It is to observe that proposals to regulate this arms
trade constitute yet another effort to manipulate only one factor in
a complex security framework constructed by nations who think
themselves the best judges of their own security needs. Their
governments, like that of India, react sharply against the paternal-
ism of outsiders who try to impose their own preferences, so that

well-meaning Westerners who would direct Third World countries into approved strategic channels are in danger of emulating the Boy Scout who helped the old lady across a road she did not want to cross. They are also incidentally encouraging an indigenous Third World arms industry that has grown 500 per cent in the last decade in reaction to the possible imposition of Western embargoes. Such embargoes themselves have unintended effects: the Western effort to curb arms in the Middle East after 1950 producing the Czech and Soviet penetration of that market just before Suez, and the American effort to restrict supersonic jet sales in Latin America giving France the chance to open up a brisk trade.[11]

I am not, of course, arguing in favour of encouraging every oil-rich ruler to seek fulfilment in military ostentation. I am saying once more that we should take a modest view of our own understanding before we tamper with complex security systems on the basis of debatable general principles.

So far, I imagine, I have appeared to be pouring cold water on the idea of arms control. The metaphor is tempting, considering all the waste heat the subject generates these days. By pointing out some of the difficulties and limitations of arms control, however, it is not my intention to debunk it. Rather, I want to suggest that its undoubted potential can only be realized by providing a sound and realistic footing. If the inherent limitations of arms control are ignored, then the defects of specific proposals may be too lightly dismissed on the grounds that the ultimate prize of a disarmed world justifies a few risks. This is happening with the current negotiations over theatre nuclear weapons, where the unattainable vision of a Europe free from nuclear danger – and even a Europe with no nuclear weapons based in it, would not be that – fosters uncritical enthusiasm for any intermediate proposal.

Policies labelled 'arms control' should be scrutinized as carefully as any other proposal to adjust the military balance. Equally, however, we should not reject an arms-control measure merely because it is modest, or not simplistically in accord with the idea of *disar*mament. Indeed, I believe that as people come to appreciate the difficulty of reconciling the internal complexity of the modern military scene with the over-simplification and rigidity often required by diplomatic negotiation, we may see a shift in arms control from what we might call 'inputs' to 'outputs'. We begin to realize that exactly what weapons the enemy has is less important than what capabilities they derive from them. So long as a nuclear power does not have a clear first-strike capability, for instance, it matters little whether it buys this or that missile. A mutual agreement to avoid such overall effects and to maintain a dialogue about the subject may be more practical in the long run than trying to achieve the same result by an endless scurrying to outlaw each new device that was not thought of in the previous agreement. The shift towards so-called 'freedom to mix' within negotiated ceilings on armaments is a faltering step in this direction. In Europe, the shift in the force-reduction talks from force ceilings to what are called 'confidence-building measures' may be another such move.[12]

The legitimacy that the idea of arms control has conferred on international dialogue about such matters is one of its most valuable contributions to making the military balance safer. Perhaps the most important contribution of all is to disseminate a wide sense of caution and restraint in confrontations between the nuclear powers. This sense of caution is the strong but narrow basis on which the nuclear weapon may yet enable us to build strategic moderation more firmly than our predecessors. The sense of confidence and mutual understanding which may exist between adversaries for the purpose of averting catastrophe will do so, however, only if we do not allow the rhetoric of arms control to make us neglect the underlying balance of power that creates our common interest in the first place. The caution that arms control requires and facilitates needs to be observed as much in avoiding complacency as in avoiding provocation.

6 The Endless Search for Safety

The Endless Search
for Safety

Most of us alive today have passed by far the greater part of our adult life in the so-called nuclear age. This makes it all too easy for us to forget how little experience we have had of this radically new strategic world. Some time ago, an eminent scientist – once one of the highest officials in the British defence establishment – was kindly trying to make an inroad, however shallow, into my obvious incapacity to appreciate the vastness of the Universe. 'Think of this,' he urged me. 'If the world were reduced to the size of a football, the oceans would scarcely make it feel damp.' We need a metaphor like that, I feel, to make us realize how early we live in the nuclear age when measured on the scale of history. With such a reminder, we may observe a decent humility about the diagnoses we make and the prescriptions we offer.

The danger of overconfidence in one's own analysis is aggravated by a surprising familiarity in the superficial appearance of the contemporary strategic world. If we look around, we see alliances, wars, threats of war, subversion and, let us not fail to notice, a good deal of what passes for peace. Over it all, however, looms the nuclear weapon; at once our greatest danger and yet, at the same time, the main basis – negative, narrow, but compelling – for hope of outdoing our predecessors in the control of arms and limitation of war.

There are, of course, those who perceive a more benign foundation for peace. As I recalled in an earlier lecture, the Western world has for several centuries cherished the hope that the benefits of science, industry and commerce would wean men away from war, which they would renounce on grounds of simple unprofitability. Indeed, might not such enlightened self-interest be reinforced by the more altruistic motives of goodwill and good neighbourliness cherished at least theoretically in the ideologies of most modern societies?

Aspirations of this kind and the increasing destructiveness of modern industrial war have inspired codes of international conduct, evolving from the Concert of Europe and the Hague Conferences, by way of the League of Nations, to the ultimate near-universal renunciation of aggressive war in the Charter of the United Nations. For all the hypocrisy with which this pledge is undertaken, cited and flouted, for all that it seems to be very much 'conflict as usual' under the veil of the Charter, I would not utterly dismiss the significance of so many nations paying at least lip-service to peace and undertaking to eschew war. The need to justify behaviour against this higher standard has a discernible if modest influence on policy. The machinery that the United Nations provides for appealing to this standard and the framework it provides for nations who want to preserve international peace and order, have made a discernible difference to world politics.[1]

There are even parts of the international community where a much more radical transformation may have overtaken the classical nation-state system. Some believe that the so-called Western or Atlantic nations have come to constitute a 'security community': that is, a group of states between whom war has become unthinkable and who therefore no longer need to take security precautions against each other. This model inspires hope of similar evolution among such much more embryonic groupings as the Organization of African Unity or the Association of South East Asian Nations.[2]

Once again, I do not think that this evolution is entirely imaginary. I do believe that Canada's confidence that she will not be invaded by the United States, for instance, is different and justifiably so, from the faith Finland can repose in its relationship with the Soviet Union. The transformation of Franco-German relations from chronic enmity to intimate mutual collaboration is deservedly one of the wonders of recent diplomacy. And yet, I fear we should view even these achievements as merely provisional, and consequently moderate all the more our expectations of rapidly extending harmony of this kind elsewhere.

I know few Frenchmen who do not believe their national nuclear force is a source of confidence to them as they contemplate the relentless resurgence of German power. I even know very senior

Canadian officials who assure me they work on the hypothesis that, if they did not freely offer military facilities to the United States, the Americans would seize them if a crisis made that seem necessary. But above all these particular doubts, we must not overlook the fact that, if harmony and co-operation have blossomed within the West during the postwar years, they have done so in the classic conditions for such behaviour – the perception of a common external enemy.

I do not suggest the community we have built is inevitably transient or that the processes at work may not have deep and healthy roots; merely that even among our Western selves it is premature to take the absence of security problems for granted. Still less, then, can we assume that our limited success is a model the rest of the world will follow. In the world at large, the peace we enjoy is of that provisional kind that, as Thomas Hobbes so well explained, we are compelled to treat as a kind of suspended war; looking to our defences for lack of complete assurance we need not do so.[3] Failing the peace of perfect understanding, we have to create a kind of synthetic substitute, by balancing and adjusting power so that, if war remains all too thinkable, it is never in anyone's immediate interest to start one.

That may be thought too gloomy a view of the world, but I am sure it is the best light we can throw on the East-West rivalry that dominates the contemporary strategic scene. I doubt whether one can have – it will certainly be immensely difficult to achieve – a relationship of trust with a power like the Soviet Union that combines a Bolshevik's dialectical view of politics with a Russian's experience of alternate vulnerability and self-aggrandisement. The fact that we can negotiate with the Soviet Union, reach mutually advantageous agreements on arms control and even make occasional provisional settlements of political differences, does not alter a fundamentally antagonistic relationship – a relationship, moreover, in which military power plays a fundamental part.

This is no mere Cold War judgement of my own. It is the consistently expressed view of the Soviet Union itself, made freely available to anyone not content to accept only the propaganda aimed at foreign audiences. Thus in a fairly recent work, crisply entitled *The Philosophical Heritage of V. I. Lenin and Problems of Contemporary War*, Lenin himself is cited approvingly for having laid it down that 'no talks, no agreements, appeals or imprecations would stop the enemy if he was not faced with a substantial military force'. Following the same line, the editors conclude: 'The stronger we are, the stronger peace is.'[4]

Nevertheless the task of doing strategic business with such a power and establishing an equilibrium, not of harmonious purposes but of countervailing power, is far from hopeless, provided only that we play the part required of us. The Soviet Union certainly does not want a major war. The work that I have just quoted firmly declares that 'the fact that imperialism would suffer defeat if it forced a new world war on mankind, does not in any way signify that we should strive toward a military confrontation'.[5] Soviet foreign policy is unquestionably assertive, openly dedicated to spreading Communism, and less openly to extending Soviet power. At the same time, Soviet operational military doctrine is offensive, and Soviet forces are configured accordingly. But neither of these characteristics means that the Soviet Union is irrepressibly urged toward military aggression.[6] The preferred role of Soviet armed forces is to exert political pressure and hold the ring while the other overt and covert instruments of Soviet diplomacy help history do Soviet work. Opportunities are seized but big risks are preferably avoided. Indeed, in an age of deterrence, the Soviet belief that events must ripen in history and the strong Bolshevik imperative to avoid being provoked into rash or precipitate action, make the Soviet Union perhaps the ideal opponent.[7] The task of those who would oppose the Soviet Union is therefore to outdo it in peaceful competition, while maintaining the military balance that activates the Soviet sense of caution.

Throughout these lectures I have reverted to this theme that the balance of power remains the best guiding principle for strategic policy. If this prescription has a weary familiarity about it, I can only plead that, after many years in strategic studies, I have come to the conclusion that it is possible to be sensible and possible to be radically original, but rarely both at the same time.

Unfortunately, the alliance upon which the West relies to keep up its end of the balance is in one of its periodic moods of uncertainty. Differences over how to proceed and especially over what tone to observe towards the Soviet Union have been endemic in the alliance, with Europeans typically showing nervousness whenever the United States takes a tough line, and fear of having their interests neglected whenever the superpowers get together. Familiarity should not make us complacent about the present disarray, however, for some fundamental changes have undoubtedly occurred. Faced with a wealthy Europe, no longer inferior in anything but military power, the United States is less inclined to foot the bills, while the Europeans feel much less deferential to American leadership. Moreover, having tasted the tangible fruits of détente – trade, movement of people, a sense, if perhaps a false one, of safety – Europeans want to feel détente can continue; indeed, they hope that, by giving the Soviet Union vested interests in good relations, détente may be a source as well as a consequence of security.[8] More bluntly, many Europeans, especially Germans, want to appease the Soviet Union, because of its growing military strength, and would like to feel it is safe to do so, because of Soviet economic weakness.

The Soviet Union obviously does put a value on trade and technological help, and is also well aware that such a line tends to reduce Western support for military preparations. A flat refusal to try the approach would clearly cause serious division both between and within Western countries and now that the Reagan Administration has resumed negotiations, the policy of détente combined with defence is back in business. We should not forget, however, that economic and political dealings create vested interests on both sides, while military weakness is appearing only in the West. Moreover, in a crisis, the fear of aggression is a far more compelling emotion than fear of disrupted trade. Defence is thus not so much a necessary condition for détente, properly understood, but actually a part of it.

A moment ago I reverted to my belief that the only long-term answer to the otherwise natural preponderance of Soviet power in Europe is a greater degree of Western European unity and self-reliance in defence matters. I have already also expressed my relative pessimism about the prospects. For the past two decades most of the talk about European defence collaboration and virtually all of the achievement has concerned the joint production of equipment. The primary motive has of course been to save money, while helping a European defence industry to survive American competition. Many hoped, however, that these practical projects, by creating vested interests in joint ventures and providing experience of co-operation, would breed a higher form of unity. If such common interests can be created, all well and good. But in fact it seems that the practice of patching together different national and commercial consortia for each project, combined with the care states take to prevent any derogation from national self-sufficiency, precisely because these *are* defence industries, has made for negligible progress toward deeper unity.[9]

Grasping admittedly at a straw or two, may it not be that the co-ordination of European Community policy in the European security conferences, the contribution to the Sinai peace force, the foray, however unsuccessful, into the Arab–Israeli dispute under EEC auspices, the faltering steps of the European Parliament and particularly of some of its party groups into security matters – may it not be that these innovations, which are largely compelled by the need to react to specific problems at the political level, are more likely to be the way in which progress will come, if come it does? To adapt a formulation I used in a different context in my last lecture, it may be that it is by trying to reach consensus on the 'output' of security policy, rather than the material 'inputs', that a common will may emerge. If it did, I suspect the wherewithal to implement it could be cobbled together rather readily from the national military establishments.

If there is to be any evolution of a more militarily effective Europe, indeed if there is even to be continued health in the existing European–American alliance – with the customary apology to Canada, for once again omitting her in the interest of linguistic convenience – then it would be easy but wrong to underestimate the continued importance of the United Kingdom. So far in these lectures I have avoided taking a parochial view from these islands, but it would be perverse of me to say nothing of the British role.

The reduced material circumstances of this country, of which we have all become so painfully conscious recently, tend to make us overlook the peculiar value of the British contribution to the alliance. For the importance of the United Kingdom is inflated by the disabilities under which each of the other leading Western European countries labours. Italy, surprisingly staunch ally though she is, is both divided and impoverished. France has resolved the psychological problems she inherited from her defeat, by espousing an idiosyncratic egoism that incapacitates her as an ally and which she is only recently showing signs of outgrowing. The Federal Republic of Germany is exposed to Soviet military power by her position in the front line, and to Soviet political pressure, by her links with her fellow Germans in the lost territories. She is further handicapped by the memories both she and others still harbour of the Nazi era and by the legal disabilities that she accepted or had imposed on her as a consequence, such as renouncing the manufacture of nuclear weapons and forgoing a complete national chain of military command.

By contrast, the inhibitions on British defence policy have been almost exclusively those of poor economic performance.[10] The decisive steps in the United Kingdom's long recessional from a worldwide military presence and from participation in almost every form of military activity, have occurred, not as a result of strategic reappraisal – though that has usually followed as a rationalization – but as the result of economic crisis. Free of more specific hindrances, Britain has been able to play the perhaps unexciting but immensely valuable role of 'most reliable ally', dutifully trying to mend transatlantic differences and playing her part, however reduced, in every dimension of alliance affairs. For Britain to abandon this role would deal the alliance a devastating blow. I doubt if we can afford more than one France. French independence, as President de Gaulle well knew, depends on the American umbrella and the German shield. It is at best debatable whether either could survive British defection. Even without its progressive economic weakness, Britain never had the power to maintain the Western coalition singlehanded; it may well be, however, that she has the power to destroy it.

Recent opinion polls reveal that only a very few of the British public favour leaving NATO. Rather more, however, support policies that might well be incompatible with that coalition's survival.[11] For myself, I would single out three policies that should not be abandoned without the gravest reflection: the nuclear force, the contribution to the Central Front, and a capacity, however modest, to undertake action outside the North Atlantic Treaty area.

The nuclear force is by far the most controversial, but there is little to add to arguments already exhaustively debated.[12] For myself, I find persuasive the argument that the existence of an ultimate centre of decision, independent of the United States, capable of launching an attack on the Soviet Union if a nuclear war in Europe began to get out of hand and to threaten British survival – that the existence of such a capability is a powerful added deterrent to Soviet aggression and to the use of the Soviet Union's massive theatre nuclear forces if aggression did occur. I am well aware of

85

objections to this theory based on the gross disparities between the Soviet Union and the United Kingdom with regard both to the destructive power of the respective nuclear forces and the vulnerability of the two nations to attack. But to confer a useful role on the British nuclear force it is not necessary to envisage its use until the United Kingdom is already under nuclear attack. At such a point, the frailty of Britain as a target system becomes almost a positive factor in enhancing the credibility of British retaliation. Given the imponderables involved and the impossibility of the Soviet Union confidently assessing the limits of British tolerance of damage and determination to retaliate, the only prudent Soviet course would be to leave a nuclear Britain unscathed by nuclear attack.

Whether the nuclear capability should be provided by the Trident missile I am not fully qualified to judge, and the problem would take us into more detail than I have time to develop. It is clear that if the rationale for a British force that I have just summarized has any validity, the force itself must not, by its vulnerability and its basing, actually provide an incentive for a nuclear attack on Britain. Trident passes that test well. It is, as usual in Britain, the question of cost that raises the most doubt. We must recognize, however, that for what they offer – assuming you accept the rationale in the first place – nuclear weapons are relatively cheap, and if Trident is difficult to fit into the defence budget, it is largely because of the immensely costly nature of the conventional forces. The Trident programme is of the same order of expense as the current Anglo-German Tornado aircraft programme; just as the much-debated new Polaris re-entry vehicle, Chevaline, costing around a thousand million pounds, has still only been a little more expensive than the Royal Navy's effort to develop a new torpedo.

If you believe in a national nuclear force – and a clear majority of the British public apparently do – it offers a much more distinctive increment of power than any comparable investment in conventional forces. Moreover a British nuclear capability, however provided, keeps a nuclear competence in European hands that are not systematically dedicated, as are the French, to refusing full collaboration with the United States. This might prove to be of no small importance if Europe is ever to move toward autonomy without a dangerous hiatus between the period of independence and the period of continued reliance on the United States. Meanwhile, many European members of NATO – more than are always willing to air their views publicly – have come to value the existence of the British force both for its present deterrent effect and its future political potential.

As I freely acknowledged in my third lecture, devoted to European defence, and as the preceding argument suggests, neither the British nor the American nuclear forces make strategic sense without an underlying framework of conventional capability. By far the most demanding task here is the maintenance of a substantial presence on the Central Front. The political, almost symbolic, reasons for this are not much less important than the strictly strategic rationale. Of course, there *are* urgent air and ground missions for British forces to perform, and if withdrawn the gap they would leave would be hard to fill. Indeed it is likely that such a withdrawal would materially shorten the fuse of nuclear escalation. But on strictly military grounds I have long believed a more rational division of labour would free Britain to concentrate on the maritime role which no other ally is so fitted to perform. But unless a more coherent European defence community creates the necessary mutual confidence to permit such a rational allocation of tasks, including a full French participation, I fear the case for a strong British presence to reassure West Germany, satisfy the United States, and display a deterrent unity to the Soviet Union, is inescapable. Moreover, believer in maritime power though I am, and while I accept that to have no provision for the renewed Battle of the Atlantic is to run a serious risk (always entailed when a possible contingency is left unprovided for), such a prolonged European war does seem increasingly less likely. The more probable eventualities are either a swift land and air battle, leading to a quick Soviet victory, or a repulse for the Soviet Union and a peace negotiated under fear of nuclear escalation.[13]

The defence review of 1981 reduced British naval forces, but only to a moderate degree if we take as our yardstick not the existing nominal size of the fleet but the depleted state of repair and readiness that had resulted from trying to make too little go too far. It may well be that a much more effective navy could rise from the remains of the old. It is to be hoped that it does, for there are certainly limits beyond which the sacrifice of maritime capability to the Central Front should not go. One such limit is the preservation of a sufficient core of naval power and prestige for Britain to play its appropriate maritime part in any more integrated European defence of the future. Another is the continued capacity, modest though it needs must be, to take a hand in military confrontations beyond the North Atlantic Treaty area.

Britain's power to mount such operations – which are, of course, by no means necessarily naval – can only be slight. But as I argued in the lecture I devoted to the affairs of the Third World, the role of Western forces there must often be subordinate to broader political and economic influences. When the Soviet Union is heavily committed, only American power will suffice, but its application may well be facilitated by the presence of some partner, however slim the material contribution. In other cases, even symbolic forces may have a useful catalytic effect: stiffening local resistance, as in Oman, or lubricating local political processes, as in Zimbabwe. As those cases remind us, Britain has a fund of experience and connection that is not yet wholly exhausted. Whether to draw on those funds, whether to intervene at all, whether to support or dissent from the policies of the United States or other British allies, are matters for judgement case by case; to have no capacity to act, pre-empts any such judgement. Recent opinion polls suggest that a majority of the British public would regret such a definitive contraction of British capabilities.[14]

It is, indeed, to the matter of public opinion that I wish to devote the last few pages of these lectures. The argument that is raging over strategy in the Western alliance is serious in every sense of the word. Some unilateralists, I suspect, are less concerned to advocate a solution to the world's strategic problems than to ensure their own hands are clean. Similarly, I fancy that many alleged multilateralists are less convinced of the virtues of any kind of disarmament, than eager to scotch unilateralism. But for all that, there are many responsible arguments on both sides of the fence that deserve a careful hearing.

As I have delivered these lectures, I have naturally been all too well aware of how forcibly many people disagree with some or all of the views I have expressed. Deeply convinced though I am myself of the errors of unilateralism, I have misgivings about the way it tends to be rebutted. It is not sufficient, indeed it is not very effective, to respond with glossier brochures depicting the strength of Soviet forces. Necessary though it is to explain that aspect of the problem, it is equally essential to rebut false remedies, and in some detail, and this not merely for effect but because we are, after all, ultimately seeking solutions to the problems of war and peace that transcend the immediate exigencies of the Cold War. If I have devoted some of the brief space available to attacking some of the sacred cows of the less inhibited disarmers, I have done so not out of contempt but out of a due appreciation of their influence and importance.

As democrats we cannot regret free discussion and as rational beings we should not reject the deeper understanding that can arise from the clash of even apparently irreconcilable ideas. Realistically we must recognize, however, that if only one side in an international conflict permits such pluralism, it pays a price, and that price will be higher, the more illusions the democratic public harbours.

To one persuaded like me of the need for vigorous defensive efforts, the most obvious price exacted by a strong pacifist movement is the detraction from military preparedness. But unjustified optimism about the strategic world can actually encourage policies that the disarmers would themselves condemn. The crowning example of this is, I suppose, the tendency for parsimony in military spending to drive strategy toward cheap and dangerous nuclear solutions in the way typified above all by the doctrine of Massive Retaliation. In an influential article published some months ago, Professor Michael Howard pointed out that a public unwilling to pay for conventional defence was hardly promising material to sit out a limited nuclear war.[15] The undoubted truth of the observation should not make us forget, however, that it is precisely the refusal to pay that has driven us so far toward dependence on nuclear weapons.

There are also more specific and technical ways in which public unwillingness to contemplate the needs of defence and admit the danger of war can foster additional dangers. The defensive capability of NATO forces on the Central Front could be cheaply and easily enhanced, for example, if the German government did not feel inhibited from permitting the preparation of fortifications and obstacles in peacetime. Our own reluctance to take civil defence seriously is rather similar.

Public attitudes can also inhibit less tangible ways of increasing our readiness for defence. The military history of this century is replete with examples of successful surprise attacks, a type of operation much favoured in Soviet military doctrine and for which Soviet forces are increasingly well adapted.[16] The decisive surprises have not, however, usually taken the simple form that those who have not studied the problem usually suppose. As the Israeli disasters early in the Yom Kippur War of 1973 illustrated very well, surprise usually consists, not of the absence of warning, but of failing to heed the warning when it comes, either because it is filtered through over-optimistic preconceptions or because the appropriate pre-cautions are politically impossible. In NATO today, the sensitivity of public opinion to anything that could be called provocative, the distaste for reminders that war might come, and the unavoidable need to orchestrate all these elements across more than a dozen sovereign publics, prevent a whole range of quite practicable im-provements in strategic responsiveness.

There is, however, another way, perhaps most profound of all, a way deeply embedded in the liberal democratic personality, by which utopianism can increase the danger of war. Conditioned by its ideals to feel guilty about the use of force, democratic opinion is addicted to crusades: if not against some foreign foe, on whom we project all the blame for our being in conflict, then against the idea of armed force itself. Today, American public opinion, notoriously moody in this way, is on the former tack, while more and more Europeans are taking the other. The danger of such emotionalism leading to intemperate action has been amply demonstrated in the past. We badly need a more balanced approach, for only thus can we hope for the sustained and coherent policies an age of deterrence demands. Such an approach begins from the vigorous scrutiny of both the problem and the remedies proposed.

In that vein, I have always been much impressed with the Amer-ican theologian Reinhold Niebuhr's observation that a sound reli-gion requires an ultimate optimism that has entertained all the grounds for pessimism.[17] If my lectures have traversed some gloomy ground, it is with that justification in mind. That there is room for optimism, I feel sure. I find it in the fact that our present debate, if fraught with danger, is at least vigorous and open, that the bulk of British opinion still staunchly accepts the need for self-defence, that Western leaders still resist defeatist voices, and that in the Soviet Union animosity is tempered with realism. Above all, there is hope in the fact that, however many specific hopes and projects for arms-control agreements may be falsified or frustrated, the idea of control, of communication between adversaries, and of the heavy burden of self-justification that falls on anyone who takes up the sword, has deeply permeated the political climate.

Where we most need Niebuhr's leavening pessimism is to counter the illusion that we can ever escape the burdens of defence altogether, and lay down this dangerous sword for good. Justifiable in their context, such phrases as Dr Kissinger's much-publicized 'window of vulnerability'[18] obscure the fact that security is a game in which the final goal is never quite in reach. The illusion that it is, distorts our sense of practical possibilities. Security, like electricity, must be on hand when you need it. But also like electricity, it is almost impossible to store; and every generation must make its own.

Notes and Selected Further Reading

Notes

1   *The Strategic Scene*: *Fact and Fancy*

1 There are many sources offering outlines of nuclear strategies and their consequences. One of the most recent and reliable is Office of Technology Assessment, US Congress, *The Effects of Nuclear War*, published commercially by Allanheld, Osman, Montclair, New Jersey, and Croom Helm, London, 1980. More help in doing one's own calculations can be derived from S. Glasstone and P. J. Dolan, *The Effects of Nuclear Weapons* (US Dept. of Defense, 3rd edn, 1977).

2 One such example is C. S. Gray and Keith Payne, 'Victory is Possible', *Foreign Policy*, Summer 1980, pp. 14–27.

3 The definitive study of this belief is P. van den Dungen, 'Industrial Society and the End of War', Ph.D. thesis, King's College, London. F. H. Hinsley, *Power and the Pursuit of Peace* (Cambridge UP, Cambridge, 1963) is a more accessible treatment. Norman Angell's *The Great Illusion* (Heinemann, London, 1910) was a much misunderstood landmark.

4 Two extended contemporary statements of this view were W. Millis, *A World Without War* (Center for Democratic Institutions, Santa Barbara, 1961) and A. Larson, *A Warless World* (McGraw Hill, New York, 1963).

5 A phrase he coined on 7 August 1914, in articles later collected as *The War That Will End War* (London, 1914).

6 The sources for these figures are two immense volumes: B. Blechman and S. S. Kaplan, *Force Without War: U.S. Armed Force as a Political Instrument*, and S. S. Kaplan, *Diplomacy of*

Power: Soviet Armed Force as a Political Instrument (Brookings Institution, Washington DC, 1978, 1981).

7 The remark was made in the National Assembly. See also *Survival*, January 1971.

8 I have chiefly in mind H. Kissinger, *Nuclear Weapons and Foreign Policy* (Harper, New York, 1957) and H. Kahn, *On Thermonuclear War* (Princeton UP, Princeton, 1960).

9 A remark he made in the House of Commons on 1 March 1955.

10 J. Steinberg, *Yesterday's Deterrent: Tirpitz and the Birth of the German Battle Fleet* (MacDonald & Co., London, 1965).

11 J. H. Kahan, *Security in the Nuclear Age* (Brookings Institution, Washington DC, 1975), pp. 270–72. This book is one of the fullest flowerings of the 'assured destruction' school of thought.

12 And see *The Effects of Nuclear War*, cited above.

13 For such a serious study, commissioned by the US Arms Control and Disarmament Agency, see A. Wolfers *et al.*, *The United States in a Disarmed World* (Johns Hopkins Press, Baltimore, 1966). For the problem of rearmament also see T. C. Schelling, *The Stability of Total Disarmament* (Institute for Defence Analyses, Washington DC, 1961).

14 I have some bias towards 'arms control', perhaps because I was a very junior member of the exalted Harvard-MIT arms-control seminar which more or less invented the concept in the late 1950s and provided the inspiration for the Kennedy Administration initiatives, including the founding of ACDA and the Test Ban Treaty. The acknowledged crystallization of these ideas was the hefty special issue of *Daedalus*, entitled 'Arms Control', published in Fall 1960.

15 Sir Edward Grey, *Twenty-five Years, 1892–1916*, Vol. 1 (Hodder & Stoughton, London, 1925), pp. 89–90.

16 J. Kugler, A. F. K. Organski and D. Fox, 'Deterrence and the Arms Race: The Impotence of Power', *International Security*, Vol. 4, No. 4, Spring 1980, p. 128.

17 Clearly, in a full-length study these figures could be greatly extended and there are many sources for them. Two major ones are the International Institute for Strategic Studies' annual *Military Balance*, and the Stockholm International Peace Research Institute's *Annual Yearbook*. In addition I have used W. W. Kaufman, 'The Defense Budget', in J. A. Pechman *et al.*, *Setting Defense Priorities* (Brookings Institution, Washington

DC, 1980); H. S. Rowen, 'The Need for a New Analytical Framework', *International Security*, Vol. 1, Fall 1976, pp. 130-46; D. Greenwood's excellent periodic Aberdeen Studies in Defence Economics, and my own chapter in G. Flynn, *The Internal Fabric of Western Security* (Croom Helm, London, 1981), pp. 153-76. There are regular articles in the *Military Balance* on the analytical problems involved in estimating Soviet military spending. For a detailed study of the nuclear balance, see A. Wohlstetter, 'Is there a Strategic Arms Race?' and 'Rivals but no Race', *Foreign Policy*, Nos. 15, 16, 1974; and debate, rebuttal and counter-rebuttal in Nos. 18, 19 and 20.

18 G. Kennan, 'A Modest Proposal', *New York Review of Books*, 16 July 1981, pp. 14-15.

19 Carnegie Endowment, *Challenges for U.S. National Security* (Washington DC, 1981), pp. 42-3. This volume also has useful sections on the budgetary estimating problem. A good treatment of the point about quality, quantity and the imminence of war is S. P. Huntington, 'Arms Races: Prerequisites and Results', *Public Policy*, 1958.

20 Letter from 'The Conference on Nuclear War in Europe', Groningen, 22-24 April 1981, p. 2, dated February 1981.

21 The concept of accuracy is well discussed in C. J. Hudson and P. H. Haas, 'New Technologies: the Prospects', and J. Digby, 'Precision Weapons: Lowering the Risks with Aimed Shots', in J. J. Holst and U. Nerlich, *Beyond Nuclear Deterrence* (Crane Russak, New York, 1977). Of course, I am aware that increased accuracy alarms some people because it tends to negate 'hardening' as a recipe for making ICBMs invulnerable. But this purpose can be served in other ways, while, as I say in my text, one compensation for inaccuracy (up to a point) is higher-yield warheads - much higher, because increases in accuracy are roughly ten times as effective as increases in yield in producing additional blast effect at a given distance from ground zero. My main point is merely to suggest that accuracy is not, *per se*, a bad characteristic in a weapon, emphasizing at this point the desirability of reducing unintended effects.

22 In his book, *The Labour Party in Perspective* (Gollancz, London, 1937).

2   The Master Weapon

1   J. Newhouse, *Cold Dawn: The Story of SALT* (Holt, Rinehart & Winston, New York, 1973), p. 176.

2   The earliest writings of value were B. Brodie, *The Absolute Weapon* (Harcourt, New York, 1946) and J. Viner, 'The Implications of the Atomic Bomb for International Relations', *Proceedings of the American Philosophical Society*, January 1946.

3   A full presentation of this view can be found in J. Kahan's *Security in the Nuclear Age*, cited above.

4   D. Holloway, 'Military Power and Political Purpose in Soviet Policy', *Daedalus*, Fall 1980, p. 23. Mr Thompson's book is *Protest and Survive*, edited by E. P. Thompson and D. Smith (Penguin, London, 1980).

5   R. Pipes, 'Why the Soviet Union Thinks It Could Fight and Win a Nuclear War', *Commentary*, July 1977. A rebuttal is made in D. Arnett, 'Soviet Attitudes Towards Nuclear War: Do They Really Think They Could Win?', *Journal of Strategic Studies*, September 1979.

6   Thus in February 1967 Mr Kosygin said: 'I believe that defensive systems, which prevent attack, are not the cause of the arms race, but constitute a factor preventing the death of people.... Maybe an anti-missile system is more expensive than an offensive system, but it is designed not to kill people but to preserve lives.'

7   Slessor's ideas are offered in J. C. Slessor, *Strategy for the West* (Cassell, London, 1954).

8   The best review of this intellectual evolution is R. E. Osgood, *Limited War Revisited* (Westview Press, Boulder, Colorado, 1979).

9   The University of Michigan (usually referred to as the Ann Arbor) speech, delivered 16 June 1962, was printed in *Survival*, September–October 1962.

10   These doctrines are discussed in Lynn Davis, *Limited Nuclear Options* (IISS Adelphi Paper 121, 1975), and in my 'Limited Nuclear War' in M. E. Howard (ed.), *Restraints on War* (OUP, London, 1979).

11   L. Brezhnev, speech in Federal Republic of Germany, 30 August 1980 (*Pravda*, 31 August 1980); cf. speech at Alma Ata, 29 August (*Pravda*, 30 August 1981).

12 Since I wrote this lecture, an excellent (pessimistic) discussion of limited nuclear war has been published as D. Ball, *Can Nuclear War Be Controlled?* (IISS Adelphi Paper 169, 1981). See also *The Effects of Nuclear War*, cited earlier, and K. N. Lewis, 'The Prompt and Delayed Effects of Nuclear War', *Scientific American*, July 1977, pp. 27ff.

13 An excellent if now a little outdated bibliography of Soviet sources is W. F. Lee, *Soviet Sources of Military Doctrine & Strategy* (Crane, Russak, New York, 1975); a recent Soviet attack in English on American strategic thinking is H. A. Trofimenko, 'Counterforce: Illusion of a Panacea', *International Security*, Spring 1981.

3 The European Balance

1 It is difficult to select one or two references on the vast subject of Soviet foreign policy. Some of the best and most balanced treatments are to be found in *Problems of Communism*, and of recent articles I would single out Pierre Hassner, 'The Soviet Union and the Western Alliance', *Problems of Communism*, August-July 1981.

2 G. Kennan, *Russia, the Atom and the West* (OUP, London, 1958), p. 97.

3 IISS, *Military Balance, 1981-82* (London, 1981), p. 123. There are many other treatments of the military balance in Europe and, although every reader will make his own corrections for bias, the wealth of information in the US Secretary of Defense's *Annual Report* should not be overlooked.

After I delivered this lecture a correspondent chided me for not giving more detail – there was no time – and particularly for not citing the large NATO anti-tank guided weapon (ATGW) capability as an offset to Soviet tanks. President Brezhnev made the same point on his November 1981 visit to the Federal Republic. In point of fact, the large number of Western ATGW is deceptive, because many are small and ineffective against the modern Soviet tanks. Moreover they would have to be quoted against the even larger number of Warsaw Pact armoured fighting vehicles (i.e. tanks *plus* personnel carriers) and discounted for their low mobility and 'hardness'. Above all the tanks are highly mobile and choose their axis of attack, while the defensive

99

missiles have the problem of reacting by high mobility, which most do not have, or of being widely dispersed. Moreover, while we, as defenders, can console ourselves a bit by counting our ATGW, it hardly seems proper for President Brezhnev to tell us in effect, 'Don't worry about my continual increase of an already large offensive force, as I see you've made some preparations to defend yourselves'!

4 The best readily available treatments of Soviet strategy and tactics for ground warfare are the numerous writings of Professor John Erickson of the University of Edinburgh. Particularly helpful is his 'Soviet Combined Arms: Theory and Practice', Defence Studies, Edinburgh, 1980. A popular treatment is *The Soviet War Machine* (Hamlyn, London and New York, 1976). Much the most detailed public source is US Department of the Army, *Soviet Army Operations*, April 1978 (IAG-13-U-78). A Soviet view, rather over sensationalized in some Western accounts, is A. A. Sidorenko, *The Offensive* (Military Publishing House, Moscow, 1970).

5 NATO strategy is spelt out in many places, including British Defence White Papers. The most detailed account of the rethought place of tactical nuclear weapons was perhaps Dr J. Schlesinger's response to a Congressional demand, *The Theatre Nuclear Force Posture in Europe: A Report to the Congress*, 1 April 1975. Congressional anxiety had been summarized in Senator Sam Nunn, 'Policy, Troops and the NATO Alliance', *Report to the Committee on Armed Services*, 2 April 1974.

6 Quoted in R. E. Osgood, *NATO: The Entangling Alliance* (Chicago UP, Chicago, 1962), p. 258.

7 H. Kissinger, *The White House Years* (Weidenfeld, London, 1979), p. 219. The same point is made by the current US Undersecretary of Defense for Policy, F. Iklé, 'NATO's First Nuclear Use: A Deepening Trap', *Strategic Review*, Winter 1980.

8 I discuss these proposals in my 'Limited Nuclear War', cited above. Outright advocacy can be found in W. D. Bennett *et al.*, 'A Credible Nuclear Emphasis for NATO', *Orbis*, Summer 1973, and C. Gray, 'Deterrence and Defense in Europe: Revising NATO's Theatre Nuclear Posture', *Strategic Review*, September 1975. Soviet theories about theatre weapons are discussed (controversially) in J. D. Douglass, *The Soviet Theater*

Nuclear Offensive (USAF, Washington DC, 1975) and J. D. Douglass, *A Soviet Selective Targeting Strategy Toward Europe* (System Planning Corporation, Arlington, 1977).

9 *H.C. Debates*, Vol. 583, col. 410, 26 February 1958.

10 R. Shearer, September 1975. Quoted in US Congressional Research Service, *The Modernization of Nato's Large-Range Theater Nuclear Forces* (Washington, 1981; prepared by Simon Lunn), p. 13.

11 These weapons are recorded in the *Military Balance* and in the US document on *Soviet Military Power* (Washington DC, 1981). The facts are not very much in controversy; what is much disputed is how to evaluate and compare the East–West balance. As good an evaluation as is readily available, is contained in the *Military Balance, 1981-82*, pp. 126-9 (earlier treatment in the *Military Balance* is unsatisfactory). Journals and newspapers are full of alternative views. As I argue in my lecture, the fundamental change is NATO's loss of a one-time virtual monopoly of 'battlefield' weapons, formerly enjoyed at a time when the Soviet Union's 'intermediate' range missiles were thought to be vulnerable to US pre-emption (slow liquid refuelling, soft sites, etc.), too inaccurate for the Soviet Union to use without clearly crossing the line to all-out war, and even to be a mere vestige of a policy of keeping Western Europe hostage until Soviet intercontinental capability became adequate.

12 The classic development of the theoretical basis for this view is the works of T. C. Schelling, *The Strategy of Conflict* (Harvard, Cambridge, Mass., 1960) and *Arms and Influence* (Yale, New Haven, 1966).

13 The book *Beyond Nuclear Deterrence*, cited above, still offers some of the best discussion of such possibilities. See also the two IISS Adelphi Papers 144 and 145, *New Conventional Weapons and East-West Security* (1978).

14 A MORI opinion poll, commissioned by the BBC on the occasion of these lectures and conducted in October 1981, revealed 52 per cent in favour of a European defence policy, a view endorsed by no less than 46 per cent of the under-25-year-olds. An interesting straw in the wind (no more) is the report by Niels J. Haagerup, 'European Security and Defence', issued on behalf of the Liberal and Democratic Group in the European Parliament, April 1981.

4   The Strategic Dimension of the Third World

1 The 'Yom Kippur' or 'October' war between Israel and Arab states in 1973 is most frequently cited for the dramatic attrition of conventional weapons. A brilliant general study of logistics is M. van Creveld, *Supplying War: Logistics from Wallenstein to Patton* (CUP, Cambridge, 1977).

   The SIPRI *Yearbooks* and other publications give the most accessible account of the arms trade with the Third World; see also the IISS, *Military Balance*, annually, for a record of specific (known) deals.

2 A very balanced analysis of the effects of a disruption of oil supplies on the world economy is 'Energy Past: An Assessment of the Foundations of U.S. Energy Policy', by L. Pugliaresi *et al.*, European-American Institute for Security Research, 1981. While sceptical about some of the more pessimistic prognoses of the future of oil supplies or of the effects of moderate disruption, the paper makes it clear that a sudden loss of Persian Gulf supplies would have very serious effects. A more anxious treatment is A. L. Alm, 'Energy Supply Interruptions and National Security', *Science*, 27 March 1981.

3 Recent studies of nuclear proliferation include J. A. Yager (ed.), *Non-proliferation and U.S. Foreign Policy* (Brookings Institution, Washington DC, 1980) and three articles in *Foreign Policy*, Fall 1979: L. Dunn, 'Half Past India's Bang', M. Brennan, 'Carter's Bungled Promise', and J. S. Nye, 'We Tried Harder (And Did More)'. See also T. B. Gati, *Soviet Perspectives on Nuclear Non-proliferation* (California Seminar on Arms Control, Paper 66, Santa Monica, November 1975).

4 A recent discussion of this view (indeed, it appeared after these lectures were delivered) is K. N. Waltz, *The Spread of Nuclear Weapons: More May be Better* (IISS Adelphi Paper 171, 1981).

5 After I delivered this lecture, I received complaints that I had *advocated* a unilateral Israeli nuclear capability against Arab states. The reader can see I did not do this, but merely reminded my listeners that friends of Israel could doubtless produce a rationale for such a force – indeed often do – and that therefore universal non-proliferation is not endorsed by all.

6 See R. Burt, *Nuclear Proliferation and Conventional Arms*

Transfers: the Missing Link (California Seminar on Arms Control, Paper 76, Santa Monica, September 1977).

7 The literature on the wars in Southeast Asia and their consequences is immense. A classic statement of the British rationale for retreat was Christopher Mayhew's book, written on his resignation as Minister for the Navy, *Britain's Role Tomorrow* (Hutchinson, London, 1967); P. Darby, *British Defence Policy East of Suez, 1947–68* (OUP, London, 1973) is the chief history of Britain's retreat. Osgood, *Limited War Revisited*, constitutes a brief account of the course of American thought on intervention. The recent reappraisal, including the Rapid Deployment Force, has yet to be thoroughly evaluated – it is, in fact, still in progress.

8 There are many studies of Soviet 'power projection'. One of the most interesting, perhaps the more so for having preceded the more dramatic events in Afghanistan and so on, is A. Hasselkorn, *The Evolution of Soviet Security Strategy 1965–75* (Crane, Russak, New York, 1978). There are several interesting articles in the IISS Adelphi Papers 151 and 152, *Prospects of Soviet Power in the 1980s* (1979).

9 Speech to Polish Communist Party Congress, 12 February 1980, Moscow Radio.

10 A. A. Grechko, 'The Leading Role of the CPSU in Building the Army of a Developed Socialist Society', *Voprosy Istorii KPSS*, May 1974, quoted in H. Gelman, *The Politburo's Management of its America Problem* (Rand, Santa Monica, 1981), p. 24.

11 See Gelman, *The Politburo*, cited above, and H. Sonnenfeldt and W. G. Hyland, *Soviet Perspectives on Security* (IISS Adelphi Paper 150, 1979).

12 Most of the studies of NATO's 'out of treaty area' problems that I have relied upon are as yet unpublished. There is a good brief critique of the Rapid Deployment Force in P. Foot, 'The Rapid Deployment Force and NATO', *Armament and Disarmament Information Report* (March/April 1981).

5 The Limitations of Arms Control

1 From the mass of works I would select H. N. Bull, *The Control of the Arms Race* (Weidenfeld, London, 1961), an early and influential treatment; E. Young's lively *A Farewell to Arms*

Control (Penguin, London, 1972); J. C. Garnett, 'Disarmament and Arms Control Since 1945', in my *Strategic Thought in the Nuclear Age* (Heinemann, London; Johns Hopkins, Baltimore, 1979); J. H. Barton and L. B. Winter, *International Arms Control: Issues and Agreements* (Stanford University Press, Stanford, 1979). There are numerous journals devoted to arms control; the Arms Control and Disarmament Research Unit of the British Foreign Office publishes a useful quarterly *Arms Control and Disarmament*, containing lists of speeches, book reviews, etc.; a valuable collection of documents is the periodically issued *Arms Control and Disarmament Agreements: Texts and Histories of Negotiations*, published by the US Arms Control and Disarmament Agency.

2 Quoted by Garnett, cited above, p. 196.

3 O. V. Bogdanov, *Razoruzhenia garentiia mira* (Moscow, 1972), p. 33 and G. A. Arbatov, *Izvestia*, 22 June 1972, quoted in S. B. Payne, *The Soviet Union and SALT* (MIT Press, Cambridge, Mass., 1980), itself a most useful book.

4 A good short study of MBFR is L. Ruehl, 'The Slippery Slope of MBFR', *Strategic Review*, Winter 1980.

5 See the rather turgid but useful J. M. Collins, *American and Soviet Military Trends Since the Cuban Missile Crisis* (Center for International Studies, Georgetown, 1978) and, of course, the *Military Balance*, SIPRI, etc.

6 *Pravda*, 7 July 1968.

7 An enthusiastic analysis of a complete test ban treaty is H. York and G. A. Greb, *The Comprehensive Nuclear Test Ban*, California Seminar on Arms Control, Paper 84, Santa Monica, June 1979.

8 A. A. Grechko, *Pravda*, 3 April 1971. See also A. Wohlstetter, 'Racing Forward or Ambling Back', *Survey*, 3/4, 1976.

9 Quoted in R. Betts, 'The Tragi-Comedy of Arms Trade Control', *International Security*, Summer 1980, p. 86.

10 For further discussion and sources, see Betts, cited above.

11 I offer a brief and now dated (in facts if not theory) discussion in L. W. Martin, *Arms and Strategy* (Weidenfeld, London; McKay, New York, 1973). See the twin IISS Adelphi Papers, *The Diffusion of Power*, Nos. 133 and 134 (1977).

12 See, *inter alia*, C. Bertram, *Arms Control and Technological Change* (IISS Adelphi Paper 146, 1978).

6   *The Endless Search for Safety*

1 A graceful and penetrating essay on this theme is F. H. Hinsley, 'Reflections on the Debate about the Nuclear Weapons', *Cambridge Review*, February 1981.

2 The idea of a 'security community' and the proposition that the Atlantic World might be one, was proposed in K. W. Deutsch *et al.*, *Political Community and the North Atlantic Area* (Princeton UP, Princeton, 1957).

3 The classic passage is: 'For war, consisteth not in battle only, or the act of fighting, but in a tract of time, wherein the will to contend by battle is sufficiently known: and therefore the notion of *time* is to be considered in the nature of war; as it is in the nature of weather. For as the nature of foul weather, lieth not in a shower or two of rain, but in an inclination thereto of many days together: so the nature of war, consisteth not in actual fighting; but in a known disposition thereto, during all the time there is no assurance to the contrary.' 'Leviathan', *The English Works of Thomas Hobbes* (John Bohn, London, 1841), Vol. 3, p. 111.

4 A. S. Milovidov and V. G. Koslov, *The Philosophical Heritage of V. I. Lenin and Problems of Contemporary War* (Military Publishing House, Moscow, 1972), pp. 20, 262.

5 Ibid., p. 18.

6 On this, see P. Hassner, 'The Soviet Union and the Western Alliance', cited above, and his paper for the 1981 IISS Conference, which will be published in due course, entitled 'American Policy Towards the Soviet Union in the 1980s: Objectives and Uncertainties'.

7 The classic study of Bolshevik operational principles and their psycho-historical roots, is N. Leites, *A Study of Bolshevism* (Free Press, Glencoe, 1953). A more modern treatment might be more inclined to dwell on the inherent sources of Soviet caution, but the book remains a valuable introduction to an understanding of Soviet strategy.

8 K. Kaiser, D. Watt *et al.*, *Western Security* (Royal Institute of International Affairs, London, 1981).

9 See, among a vast array of literature, the series of Adelphi Papers with overall title 'The Alliance and Europe'.

10 See my 'The Domestic Context of British Defence Policy', in

G. Flynn, *The Internal Fabric of Western Security*, cited above. The other 'country studies' in this volume – France (Yves Laulan), Germany (Josef Joffe) and Italy (Stefano Silvestri) – would be a useful basis for judgement on the comparative remarks I make so abruptly in the previous paragraph.

11 The MORI opinion poll, referred to in note 14 on page 101, revealed that only 9 per cent favoured withdrawal from NATO. 52 per cent were in favour of a national nuclear force.

12 A brief treatment is L. Freedman, *Britain and Nuclear Weapons* (Macmillan, London, 1980). See also P. Nailor and J. Alford, *The Future of Britain's Deterrent Force* (IISS Adelphi Paper 156, 1980); and House of Commons Defence Committee, 4th Report, 1980-81, *Strategic Nuclear Weapons Policy*.

13 See the excellent analysis of D. Greenwood, cited earlier, especially 'Reshaping Britain's Defences', *Aberdeen Studies in Defence Economics*, Summer 1981, and his useful series of articles in *The Times*, 27-30 October 1981.

14 A well written and documented study of British defence policy reaching very different conclusions from mine is D. Smith, *The Defence of the Realm in the 1980s* (Croom Helm, London, 1980).

15 M. Howard, 'The Forgotten Dimensions of Strategy', *Foreign Affairs*, Summer 1979, p. 963.

16 There is now extensive literature on surprise and 'threat perception'. See K. Knorr, 'Strategic Intelligence: Problems and Remedies', in my *Strategic Thought in the Nuclear Age*, cited earlier; and K. Knorr, 'Threat Perception', in Knorr, *Historical Dimensions of National Security Problems* (Kansas UP, Wichita, 1976); also R. Godson (ed.), *Intelligence Requirements for the 1980s* (Transaction Books, New Brunswick and London, 1980).

17 I am sorry to say that I cannot now find the reference to this statement of Niebuhr's which I first paraphrased in a book *Peace without Victory*, nearly twenty-five years ago, in which I carelessly also failed to provide a precise citation.

18 The phrase he used (which was widely quoted, but which does not appear in the authorized text of his remarks) at a conference in Brussels in 1979. The text can be found in *Washington Quarterly*, Autumn 1979.

Selected Further Reading

A large number of suggestions for further reading on specific topics is included in the notes to the lectures. The following list contains some books of rather more general interest. I have used my own judgement in their selection, some being included to represent a point of view, not always my own, and others to provide what I would regard as a judicious introduction to strategic studies. For facts, the best two sources are the IISS's *Military Balance* and the SIPRI *Yearbooks*. For periodic analysis, the most useful journals for the type of question I address in these lectures are *Survival* (IISS, London); *International Security* (Center for Science and International Affairs, Harvard); *Foreign Policy* (Carnegie Endowment, Washington); *Washington Quarterly* (Center for Strategic and International Studies, Georgetown DC); *ADIU Report* (Armament and Disarmament Information Unit, University of Sussex).

Valuable series of pamphlets or smaller books are the IISS's *Adelphi Papers*, the Georgetown Center's *Washington Papers*, and the California Seminar on Arms Control's *Discussion Papers*.

H. Amirsadeghi (ed.), *The Security of the Persian Gulf* (Croom Helm, London, 1981)

J. H. Barton and L. D. Weiler, *International Arms Control* (Stanford UP, Stanford, 1976)

J. Baylis (ed.), *British Defence Policy in a Changing World* (Croom Helm, London, 1977)

B. Blechman and S. S. Kaplan, *Force without War, U.S. Armed Force as a Political Instrument* (Brookings Institution, Washington DC, 1978)

H. N. Bull, *The Control of the Arms Race* (Weidenfeld, London, 1961)

G. Flynn *et al.*, *The Internal Fabric of Western Security* (Croom Helm, London, 1981)

L. Freedman, *The Evolution of Nuclear Strategy* (Macmillan, London, 1981)

A. A. Grechko, *The Armed Forces of the Soviet State* (Military Publishing House, Moscow, 1975; USAF translation, Govt. Printing Office, Washington DC, 1975)

J. J. Holst and U. Nerlich (eds), *Beyond Nuclear Deterrence* (Crane, Russak, New York, 1977)

M. E. Howard, *Restraints on War: Studies in the Limitation of Armed Conflict* (OUP, Oxford, 1979)

S. S. Kaplan, *Diplomacy of Power: Soviet Armed Force as a Political Instrument* (Brookings Institution, Washington DC, 1981)

Laurence Martin *et al.*, *Strategic Thought in the Nuclear Age* (Heinemann, London; Johns Hopkins, Baltimore, 1979)

T. B. Miller, *The East–West Strategic Balance* (Allen and Unwin, London, 1981)

R. E. Osgood and R. W. Tucker, *Force, Order and Justice* (Johns Hopkins, Baltimore, 1967)

R. E. Osgood, *Limited War Revisited* (Westview Press, Boulder, Colorado, 1979)

V. D. Sokolovsky, *Soviet Military Strategy*, 3rd edn (Crane, Russak, New York, 1975)

E. P. Thompson and D. Smith, *Protest and Survive* (Penguin, London, 1980)

US Arms Control and Disarmament Agency, *Arms Control and Disarmament Agreements* (US ACDA, Washington DC, periodically published)